THE PACIFIC RIM EXPLORER

EXPLORER

THE·COMPLETE·GUIDE

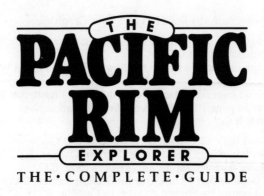

BRUCE OBEE

WITH MAPS BY
JANET BARWELL-CLARKE

WHITECAP BOOKS

Cover photographs by Bob Herger, Photo/Graphics

All photographs, except those on pages 63, 92 and 185 by Bruce Obee, Brentwood Bay, B.C.
Photograph on page 63 by Jim Darling of the West Coast Whale Research Foundation.
Photograph on page 92 by Janet Barwell-Clarke, Brentwood Bay, B.C.
Photograph on page 185 by Dr. Ivor Barwell-Clarke, New Westminster, B.C.

Maps by Janet Barwell-Clarke, Brentwood Bay, B.C.
Chapter head drawings by Suzanne Gagnon, Ganges, B.C.
Typesetting by Alston Graphic Services, Victoria, B.C.
Cover and book design by Silk Questo Design, Sidney, B.C.
Printed and bound by Friesen Printers in Canada.

Canadian Cataloguing in Publication Data

Obee, Bruce, 1951-
    The Pacific Rim explorer

        Includes index.
        Bibliography: p.
        ISBN 0-920620-77-9

        1. Vancouver Island (B.C.) — Description and travel
    — Guide-books. 2. Pacific Rim National Park (B.C.) —
    Guide-books. I. Title.
    FC3844.2.O24 1986   917.11'34   C86-0911411

First Edition 1986
Published by Whitecap Books, 1086 West 3rd Street,
North Vancouver, B.C. V7P 3J6

For Janet,
my children's mother,
who so generously shares
her wisdom and love

BY THE SAME AUTHOR

The Gulf Islands Explorer — The Complete Guide

CONTENTS

LIST OF MAPS

THANKS TO . . .

Howie Hambleton, Bill McIntyre and the others from Pacific Rim National Park for helping get it right . . . to Dr. Jim Haggarty of the B.C. Provincial Museum, Peter Olesiuk and Dr. Michael Bigg of the Pacific Biological Station, and Jim Darling of the West Coast Whale Research Foundation . . . to friend and fishing expert Jim Gilbert, to George Robinson and his son Michael Burgess for hiking at dawn . . . to Debbie Burgess and Karen Fitzgerald for giving me some time . . . to Eric Robinson, Cara and Matthew Obee, Nicole and Lauren Obee for taking us camping on the coast . . . and to my little brother, Eric, who steers a steady ship.

INTRODUCTION

The first time I saw Long Beach we came around a bend in the road and it was suddenly there. The morning sun was beating down on the longest stretch of sand I'd ever seen: breakers were sliding up the beach and foaming around an enormous rock at the edge of the sea.

I'd been raised on the tamer beaches of Victoria, where the sea and its ever-changing moods became as much a part of me as my blood and bones. I was brought up to believe there was no scenery to match the seashore at home. But in finding Long Beach I discovered the most beautiful place on earth, and though I stepped onto the sand with the confidence of a well-heeled beach rat, I felt intimidated by its vastness.

There was more, I was told, so I gathered my gear and set out on the West Coast Trail. As I hiked out of the rain off a mucky trail I swore I'd never do it again. But as time passed, the West Coast Trail, like Long Beach, became a memory to relive.

Then I nearly broke my back on the horrible portages of the Nitinat Lakes. I vowed never to return, but somewhere in my memory I heard fish jumping in the morning mist over Hobiton Lake and I went back for more of the same punishment.

I began traveling the Broken Group Islands of Barkley Sound, exploring the intricate shorelines, the sea caves and sea lion haul-outs by inflatable boat. But always, as we buzzed from bay to cove, from island to reef, I felt an irresistible urge to travel it all by canoe. So I started touring the Broken Group at the leisurely pace of the paddler, like the Indians of Barkley Sound had done for thousands of years before me.

Now others, like myself, have begun to discover the rugged beauty, the challenges and the uniqueness of Pacific Rim. And as I watch my two little daughters digging in the sand, jumping the waves and roasting marshmallows on the campfire, I'm grateful for two good excuses to explore it all again.

Brentwood Bay, British Columbia
March, 1986

Bruce Obee

WHEN A PARK IS NOT A PARK

On April 2, 1969 the British Columbia legislature passed the West Coast National Park Act, setting in motion the bureaucratic process of establishing a national park on the southwest coast of Vancouver Island. Seventeen years later, as the first edition of *The Pacific Rim Explorer* went to press, that national park still had not been legally established.

Under an agreement accompanying the legislation, the British Columbia government was to acquire all of the lands for Pacific Rim National Park and equally share the costs with Canada's federal government. Originally, the agreement stipulated that land acquisitions in the Long Beach and Broken Group Islands sections of the park were to be completed by 1974 and the West Coast Trail properties were to be acquired by the following year. Numerous amendments to the agreement, however, altered those deadlines.

The main stumbling block has been forest lands. Logging companies with tree farm licences in the Pacific Rim National Park area were reluctant to give up their legal claims to marketable timber. They argued that although most of their holdings involved publicly owned land they should be compensated for relinquishing their rights to take the timber. They did not want cash: trees from other nearby areas were needed to provide logs for their mills in the same areas.

Shortly after the West Coast National Park Act was passed, working boundaries were established and the province began buying private properties within the boundaries. Much of the private land was acquired by 1978 when negotiators got serious about settling the question of timber rights. Complicating the difficulties with forest companies was the insistence of conservationists that the Nitinat Lakes should be included in the West Coast Trail section of the park. The original agreement did not include Nitinat but, through a well-organized campaign, environmentalists convinced the provincial government in 1972 to declare a moratorium on logging in the Nitinat area.

By August of 1985 the province and forest companies had reached a tentative agreement which was acceptable to the federal government. Two months later the provincial environment minister established a special advisory committee on wilderness preservation to examine issues concerning 24 wilderness areas throughout the province. Pacific Rim National Park was included in the 24 areas, in spite of the agreement-in-principle between the province and forest companies.

So, as 1986 began, Pacific Rim National Park still did not legally exist. Under the tentative agreement, land in the Long Beach unit, including a small picnicking area at Kennedy Lake on Highway 4, is 81 square kilometres; the West Coast Trail and Nitinat Lakes is 193 square kilometres. The land in the Broken Group Islands is 16 square kilometres. Pacific Rim differs from other national parks in that it includes parts of the ocean within its boundaries. Ocean area totals 223 square kilometres, making the entire park area 513 square kilometres.

Pacific Rim National Park has operated since the early 1970s as if it were legally a park. This book is written with the assumption that the areas within the tentative boundaries will be officially designated national parkland.

CHAPTER ONE

Pacific Rim
A LAND OF THE SEA

The Pacific Ocean is a powerful, dynamic force that influences the life of every organism that inhabits its depths and coastline. On the southwest shores of Vancouver Island it provides nourishment for migrating sea lions, whales and birds that rest at its reefs, bays and beaches; it dictates what vegetation will survive in the windlashed forests above the shores; it supplies a bountiful harvest for stalwart fishermen who pursue their vocation not only for profit, but for love of the sea.

There is nowhere on the southwest coast of Vancouver Island that the power of the Pacific Ocean cannot be felt. It is in constant motion: its tidal currents bring souvenirs from afar, treasures for beachcombers and scavengers; its rolling swells erode the craggy coast as they crash against the land, carving deep caves where cormorants and other seabirds raise their offspring; its tides sweep in and out, exposing and protecting the creatures and plants of the seashore. The motion of this sea is always audible as it gently laps at the edges of sheltered coves and lagoons, or furiously whips the headlands and beaches that face the open sea. And as conspicuous as its sounds are its fragrances — rich, refreshing mixtures of salt spray, seaweeds and rain forests.

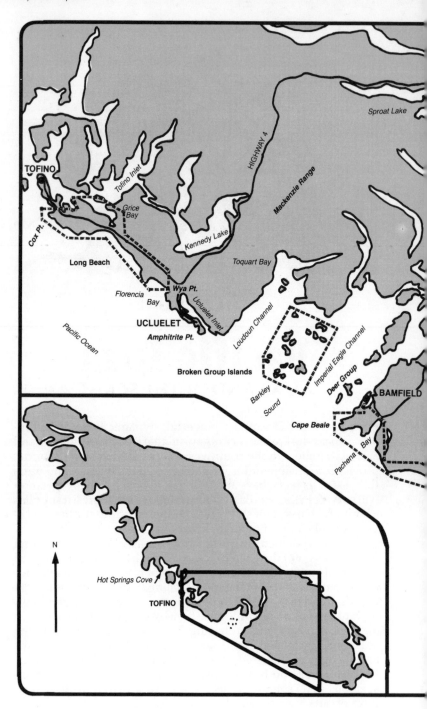

HIGHWAY 19

PARKSVILLE

Cameron Lake

PORT
ALBERNI

Alberni Inlet

HIGHWAY 1

PACIFIC RIM

YOUBOU

HIGHWAY 18

Cowichan Lake

Hobiton Lake

xslat Lake

Squalicum Lake

Nitinat Lake

West Coast Trail

PORT RENFREW

Port San Juan

HIGHWAY 14

Pacific Rim National Park Boundary ━ ━ ━ ━ ━ ━ ━ ━ ━

| 0 | 20 | 40 |

Kilometres

At one time only the hale and hearty chose to live along the rugged shores of southwest Vancouver Island, in villages like Tofino, Ucluelet or Bamfield. Their highway was the Pacific Ocean, an often inhospitable sea that could stormbind the occupants of remote villages for weeks on end. Today, with highways, ferries and airlines, these once isolated seaports have become accessible to outsiders.

Before the creation of Pacific Rim National Park there was no place on the west coast of Canada where large tracts of land and sea, representative of this magnificent area's natural features, were preserved forever as a national park. Even at Pacific Rim many of the ancient evergreens have already fallen victim to the woodman's axe. If legislation to create the park had not been passed in 1969, much of the forests at Long Beach and around the West Coast Trail and Nitinat Lakes would have been clear cut.

The establishment of Pacific Rim National Park was greeted with mixed feelings by people who had shared the area with few others in earlier decades. Many resented the intrusion, the inevitable rules and regulations required to protect the beauty that lured people here in the first place. Others saw the new park as final assurance that the spectacular scenery in this corner of Canada would remain intact for their children and grandchildren and other generations of the future.

Pacific Rim National Park encompasses a total of 513 square kilometres, but the entire southwest coast of Vancouver Island is affected by the park. Tourism has suddenly become a major industry in Tofino and Ucluelet, at opposite ends of Long Beach, and in Bamfield and Port Renfrew, at either end of the West Coast Trail. People from all parts of the world are learning through television programs, home videos, books, magazine and newspaper articles of this extraordinary place on the western edge of Canada, where they can stroll barefoot on miles of sandy beach, canoe through a maze of uninhabited islands and hike for a week beside the open sea.

The park is divided into three sections: all are similar by their association with the sea, yet they differ by the opportunities they present. Long Beach is 81 square kilometres with 30 kilometres of shoreline stretching from Cox Point in the northwest to Wya Point in the southeast. In the Broken Group, southeast of Long Beach in the middle of Barkley Sound, 100-odd islets and islands form an intricate network of sheltered waterways within an area of more than 100 square kilometres. The West Coast Trail, once a route to civilization for shipwrecked mariners, now is a challenging wilderness adventure, a 72-kilometre hike along a stretch of coast appropriately named the Graveyard of the Pacific.

The areas surrounding Pacific Rim National Park are equally

The Broken Group Islands

intriguing. The islands and hot springs beyond the village of Tofino entice boaters and kayakers searching for excitement and solitude. Barkley Sound, a total of about 800 square kilometres, is
known across the continent for its unparalleled salmon fishing.
Bamfield, on the southeast side of Barkley Sound, is a picturesque

fishing village with its homes and buildings clinging to the rocky shores of an inlet and a boardwalk running along one side. It's a starting point for hikes to sandy beaches and exposed headlands, and a home base for fishermen and scuba divers exploring the waters of Barkley Sound.

This book covers the southwest coast of Vancouver Island from Hot Springs Cove in the northwest to Port Renfrew in the southeast. Throughout the text the term "Pacific Rim" refers to this entire area, including places inside and outside Pacific Rim National Park.

TO PACIFIC RIM BY LAND, SEA OR AIR

Each of Pacific Rim National Park's three sections and the areas surrounding them are accessible by different routes. Long Beach, the most popular part of the park, can be reached by highways from all major Vancouver Island centres. Bus companies serve the villages of Tofino and Ucluelet at opposite ends of Long Beach. The *Lady Rose*, a 31-metre passenger and cargo ship based in Port Alberni, runs to Ucluelet and the Broken Group Islands from late spring to early fall. Pacific Rim Airlines, also based in Port Alberni, has scheduled flights to Ucluelet and Tofino.

Barkley Sound, southeast of Long Beach, can be reached by boat from Ucluelet, Toquart Bay, Bamfield or Port Alberni. Bamfield, on the opposite side of the sound from Ucluelet and Long Beach, is accessible by gravel logging roads from Port Alberni and Cowichan Lake. The *Lady Rose* runs year-round to Bamfield, and Pacific Rim Airlines has scheduled flights to Bamfield.

The northwest end of the West Coast Trail is reached via Bamfield. The main route to Port Renfrew, at the opposite end of the trail, is Highway 14 from Colwood, on the outskirts of Victoria.

Details on transportation to each part of Pacific Rim are provided in each chapter.

INFORMATION — HELPFUL ADVICE FOR NEWCOMERS

Tourist information centres are at conspicuous locations in all of Pacific Rim's main population centres — Port Alberni, Bamfield, Ucluelet and Tofino. Information about the services offered by these communities is available from the centres.

Pacific Rim Park has information outlets at both ends of the West Coast Trail and just inside the park boundary at Long Beach. The main centre is at Long Beach, where travelers can obtain information about any part of the park and services provided by nearby communities.

Detail on how to find information for each section of Pacific Rim Park and the areas outside the park is provided in each chapter. Addresses to write for tourist information are on p. 177.

ACCOMMODATION AND CAMPING — BOOK AHEAD

Although there's a variety of motels, resorts, lodges, hotels, campgrounds and trailer parks in the Pacific Rim area between Port Renfrew and Hot Springs Cove, it's wise to book accommodation well ahead if you're traveling between spring and autumn or on holiday weekends during the year. Reservations are not taken for federal or provincial campgrounds but some commercial campgrounds and trailer parks accept reservations. More detail on the types of accommodation available throughout Pacific Rim is provided in each chapter of this book.

The most reliable source for up-to-date accommodation listings and descriptions of services is the B.C. Ministry of Tourism's *Accommodation Guide*, which has been published annually since 1925. A million copies are printed each year and distributed to three dozen countries. Each property listed in the guide has been inspected by government "accommodation counsellors" who ensure the particular accommodation meets the ministry's standards of "comfort, courtesy and cleanliness." Those which meet the standards are given a bright blue "Approved Accommodation" sign or window decal for public display. If a resort, motel, hotel or campground is not listed in the guide it may not be up to standard: when booking a place to stay, ask if the outlet is listed in the guide, and if not, why. Some accommodations may not be listed because they are new, the proprietors failed to submit the nominal listing fee before the publication deadline, or the owner opted to be excluded. The *Accommodation Guide* is available free from tourist information centres throughout British Columbia or from provincial government agents in Port Alberni and Ucluelet. It can also be requested by writing to the Ministry of Tourism at the address on p. 177. Other accommodation information may be available from local tourist bureaus and chambers of commerce.

Most tenters begin camping on Vancouver Island's west coast around Easter weekend. Although the sun may shine for weeks at a time campers should be prepared for heavy rains at any time of year. Tenters need good flies or plastic tarps. Besides the camping areas described in each chapter, there are several campgrounds not far off the beaten track along the main access routes to the Pacific Rim area. They're good locations for vacations and handy overnight stops for people traveling to and from Pacific Rim.

Camping on Benson Island

For people traveling to Long Beach from Vancouver Island's Highway 19, there's Rathtrevor Provincial Park, four kilometres southeast of Parksville. Englishman River Park is nine kilometres southwest of Parksville, off Highway 4, and Little Qualicum Falls Park is l9 kilometres west of Parksville, off Highway 4. In the Port Alberni area there are provincial campgrounds at Sproat Lake, 13 kilometres northwest of Port Alberni, and at Stamp Falls, 14 kilometres north of Port Alberni. Forest companies have campgrounds off Highway 4 about halfway along the north shore of Sproat Lake and at the western end of the lake. Another forest company campground is near the Kennedy River between Sproat Lake and Long Beach.

People traveling to Barkley Sound and Bamfield from Port Alberni can camp at a forest company site on Sarita Lake.

Travelers coming to Bamfield through Lake Cowichan on Highway 18 can find several campsites on both sides of Cowichan Lake. The British Columbia Forest Service has two campgrounds on the north side of the lake near the village of Youbou, and another at Nixon Creek near Caycuse on the opposite side. There are two forest company campsites near the east end of Cowichan Lake, another about halfway along the south shore and another at the western end. Gordon Bay Provincial Park is on the south side, about 13 kilometres west of the village of Lake Cowichan. A forest company campground is also available on the east side of Nitinat Lake.

Facilities at forest company and B.C. Forest Service campgrounds are minimal but, unlike provincial parks, no camping fees are charged. All of these campsites are located in scenic surroundings.

Except where special restrictions have been imposed, it is legal to camp on crown land, including beaches. Most beaches in B.C. are public property up to the highest high tide line, which is where the driftwood sits at the top of the beach. Tides in summer are generally lower than in winter and it is possible to camp on a beach without worrying about the tide washing away your tent, or trespassing on private land. Camping is prohibited or discouraged on some beaches due to fire hazards and many beaches are inaccessible, except by boat. You can camp anywhere along the West Coast Trail but all other camping in Pacific Rim National Park is allowed only in designated areas. There are numerous beautiful camping beaches outside the park, particularly around Barkley Sound. These are wilderness sites and should be left as if you'd never been there.

Private lands, including Indian reserves, are out of bounds to campers except where their use is offered by owners.

POLICE, MEDICAL AND GOVERNMENT SERVICES

The Royal Canadian Mounted Police have detachments in Port Alberni, Ucluelet and Tofino. Each has a high-speed boat to reach areas inaccessible by road. Port Alberni RCMP are responsible for Bamfield and surrounding roads and Sooke RCMP patrol Port Renfrew at the southeast end of the West Coast Trail.

Visitors from outside B.C. should be aware that seatbelts must be worn in vehicles by law. They should also be aware of the "Counter/Attack" program, a province-wide war against impaired drivers. Roadblocks are occasionally set up to nab drunk drivers. RCMP advise tourists in the Pacific Rim area to ensure items such as coolers, campstoves, lanterns and other equipment are locked in vehicles before leaving a campsite or retiring for the night. Possessions like binoculars, cameras, wallets, watches, traveler's cheques and passports should be locked in the trunk of a car. Valuable items should never be left unattended on a beach and boaters shouldn't leave fishing gear and other equipment in unlocked boats.

Ambulance services are available to Pacific Rim communities and general hospitals are located at Port Alberni and Tofino. Ucluelet has a health clinic and Bamfield has a clinic and Red Cross Outpost.

Provincial government agents' offices are located in Port Alberni and Ucluelet. Some local topographic maps of the Pacific Rim area may be available and any maps sold by the British Columbia government can be ordered through the agents. Provincial fishing and hunting licences for both resident and nonresident sportsmen can also be purchased. Government agent offices are open during normal business hours on weekdays.

PACIFIC RIM WEATHER — WEST IS WET

The Pacific Rim area, between Port Renfrew in the southeast and Hot Springs Cove in the northwest, lies at the mercy of prevailing westerly winds which carry in great masses of warm, moist air from the open sea. Precipitation along this coast is among the heaviest in the world. Some falls as snow but most precipitation is rain. The wet season begins in late September and ends about the middle of March, although heavy rains often occur in the middle of summer. June, July and August, however, are relatively dry months, a distinct contrast from the other seasons. Thick, dark rain clouds hover over the southwest coast of Vancouver Island for days on end in autumn and winter. But there are also periods when the beaches of Pacific Rim are drenched in winter sunshine. The influence of the Pacific Ocean's warm waters is felt along the entire British Columbia coast, an area known for its mild winters and warm summers. It is also regularly hit by gales, especially during winter.

As incoming weather systems hit the mountains that form the backbone of Vancouver Island, they dump pitiless rains on the west coast villages of Tofino, Ucluelet and Bamfield. The contrasts in weather between the east and west coasts of southern Vancouver Island are astounding when one considers they're only 120 kilometres apart. Only 616 millimetres of rain falls on the British Columbia capital of Victoria each year, while Ucluelet is saturated by 3,302 millimetres — more than five times as much.

The wettest weather station in North America is at Henderson Lake, near the northeast corner of Barkley Sound, where the average annual rainfall over a 14-year period was 6,550 millimetres. Records from Henderson Lake show that on one De-

Seaside rain forests

cember day in 1926 it rained more than 415 millimetres — about two-thirds the average *annual* precipitation for Victoria. The differences in precipitation between villages on the coast are surprising. Ucluelet's 3,301.8 millimetres is 75.8 millimetres higher than the annual average for Tofino, which is only 40 kilometres to the northwest. Ucluelet also receives 448.1 millimetres more rain than Bamfield, which is 30 kilometres away on the opposite side of Barkley Sound.

In spite of the rain the southwest coast of Vancouver Island receives a generous share of sunshine. A sunshine recorder at Tofino, the only one in the Pacific Rim area, indicates that over a 30-year period the sun shone an average of 1,723.5 hours a year — 31.3 hours longer than at one weather station in Vancouver. Victoria, however, receives an average of 467.5 hours more annual sunshine than Tofino.

The following statistics are provided by the Victoria weather office of Environment Canada. They are based on many years of readings from Tofino, which enjoys, or endures, similar weather conditions to other areas along the southwest coast of Vancouver Island.

Sunshine

Average hours of bright sunshine based on readings over a 30-year period.

January	February	March	April	May	June
66.1	72.2	138.6	179.6	215.5	219.7

July	August	September	October	November	December	Year
223.8	187.8	169.9	134.1	64.1	52.1	1,723.5

Precipitation

Mean total precipitation in millimetres, based on readings over a 30-year period.

January	February	March	April	May	June
382.7	357.3	361.2	231.4	143.0	101.7

July	August	September	October	November	December	Year
86.1	114.1	163.2	391.8	429.3	464.2	3,226.0

Temperature

Mean daily temperatures in celsius, including mean daily maximum and minimum temperatures.

	Jan	Feb	Mar	Apr	May	Jun	Jul	Aug	Sept	Oct	Nov	Dec	Year
Maximum:	6.7	8.5	9.0	10.9	13.7	16.1	18.3	18.1	17.2	13.4	9.8	7.7	12.5
Minimum:	0.8	2.0	1.9	3.5	5.9	8.5	10.2	10.7	9.0	6.4	3.4	2.1	5.4
Mean:	3.8	5.3	5.5	7.2	9.9	12.4	14.2	14.4	13.1	9.9	6.6	4.9	8.9

DRESSING FOR WEST COAST WEATHER

It's the outdoors that lures people to the southwest coast of Vancouver Island: the long, sandy beaches, the rain forests and hiking trails, the fishing, canoeing and nature cruises. Nobody comes here for evenings at the theatre, for afternoons with the symphony, or to consider the epicurean endeavors of foreign chefs. So leave your tuxedo and cocktail dress at home and pack some well-worn boots and wet-weather gear.

Although the coast of British Columbia is known for its temperate climate the breezes that blow off the sea can be chilly, particularly at night. A warm jacket or vest under a windbreaker will fend off the cold in spring, summer and fall. Heavier clothing is obviously needed in winter. Bundling up and strolling the beaches of Pacific Rim during violent winter storms is invigorating for those prepared to enjoy the rain and wind. There are also summer days when the sun beats down on the beaches and you can spend from dawn to dusk lolling around in a swim suit or shorts, sauntering down to the sea's edge once in a while to cool off.

Rain clothes, regardless of the season, are as important to west coast vacationers as toothbrushes and shoes. Occasionally the sun shines on the southwest coast for days, even weeks at a time, but most who come to Long Beach, Barkley Sound or the West Coast Trail get at least a few hours of rain during their stay. An umbrella will suffice when it's calm, but on windy days they tend to blow inside-out. The quality of rain gear depends on what you intend to do. A cheap jacket and pants will do if you plan to spend most of the time combing the beaches between snoozes in a seaside cabin. More energetic types — hikers, canoeists or boaters — should pack good wet-weather clothing which isn't likely to split in the seams and tear at the elbows and knees. A hat, especially a sou'wester, is better than a hood. People who take whale-watching or nature cruises should have rain gear. If you arrive on the southwest coast unprepared for rain, wet-weather clothing is available from any of the communities.

The kind of boots and shoes to pack, like rain gear, depends on your plans. In summer you can walk the shores at Long Beach barefoot or with thongs that can be worn in the water. Sneakers may be sufficient for the hiking trails around Long Beach if the weather has been dry, but rubber or high-topped leather boots are best if there's likely to be mud on the trails. The hikes around Bamfield generally require boots.

Whether you're camping or staying in a cabin or lodge you'll likely spend most of your time outside on a west coast vacation. So, before leaving home, think about the things you may do and pack for the outdoors.

HYPOTHERMIA — THE CHILL THAT KILLS

Anyone who enjoys the outdoors — hikers, swimmers, anglers, boaters, divers, hunters, bird watchers, whale watchers — is susceptible to hypothermia. Often known as the chill that kills, hypothermia is a widely misunderstood, often ignored phenomenon that claims dozens of lives every year. In the cold waters of Pacific Rim it can snuff out a life within a couple of hours. It can overcome a hiker on a misty forest trail with little warning.

Simply defined, hypothermia is a lowering of the inner body temperature causing severely reduced blood circulation and profound impairment of normal body functions. A boater accidentally dumped into Barkley Sound or a hiker who slips into a west coast stream will begin to lose heat from the skin, or peripheral tissues, almost immediately. It takes 10 or 15 minutes, however, before the heart and brain begin to cool.

The first reaction is to shiver. Shivering is a chemical increase in energy production that raises the warmth level by approximately five times: it should never be suppressed. But in water of 10 degrees celsius, which may be common in Pacific Rim seas during summer, shivering is an inadequate form of heat production. An average 70-kilogram person will lose consciousness within about an hour and a half of the dunking when the inner body temperature drops from the normal 37 degrees to between 30 and 32 degrees. The temperature falls to about 24 degrees during the next hour, the heart fibrillates, and the misery ends. Some people, of course, live longer than others in cold water. A small child, in water of 10 degrees, could be dead within an hour while an obese person may last up to six hours because of the insulative blubber.

Although the physiological characteristics of hypothermia are the same in both water and cold air, the symptoms of approaching hypothermia in hikers are not as easily recognized. A person in the early stages of air hypothermia may not acknowledge a problem and deny having any ill feeling. He feels cold and needs exercise to warm up. He shivers and feels numb but may appear to be of sound mind, having no appreciation for the seriousness of his condition. A few moments later the shivering intensifies; it's out of control. By the time he begins to ramble incoherently his mind is sluggish. His physical coordination fails and he stumbles. He's no longer able to care for himself.

Members of an outdoor group should constantly watch each other, particularly in damp, cold weather. A general rule is to believe the symptoms, not the victim, when hypothermia is apparently taking hold.

Exercise, when possible, will help a hypothermic hiker produce body heat, but in cold water the opposite is the case. Someone who tries to swim ashore from an overturned boat cools 35 percent faster than a person who floats motionless in a life jacket. A position known as the "heat escape lessening posture (HELP)" helps retain warmth in high heat-loss areas such as the groin, neck and sides of the chest. A hypothermia victim, either floating in a life jacket or sitting on land, simply holds the arms tight against the chest sides and pulls the knees up, to reduce the flow of water or cold air over the crucial areas.

In situations where the victim needs assistance the most important task is to remove wet clothing. The primary cause of air hypothermia is dampness. Clothing becomes damp from sweat, rain or heavy dew on bushes. If it is cooled by cold air or wind, hypothermia strikes quickly.

Here are some basic treatments for hypothermia:

- Place the victim, stripped, in a sleeping bag with one, preferably two, warm people, also stripped. Skin-to-skin contact is one of the most effective rewarming methods.
- Rescuers should breathe close to the mouth and nostrils of the victim, providing warmth to the core of the body through inhalation. When possible, water should be boiled and steam directed under a makeshift hood over the hypothermic person's head.
- Apply hot, wet towels or blankets.
- Give hot, nonalcoholic drinks.
- Don't move the hypothermic person until he or she is sufficiently rewarmed. Then pack up the planned activities and go home. Never continue the hike.

Both air and water hypothermia can be worsened by complications such as injury or dehydration, but it can usually be avoided by a basic understanding of its causes, symptoms and treatments. Hikers should determine before the journey which members of their party are most susceptible and keep a close watch on those particular people. Boaters should be aware of available survival equipment such as the UVic Thermofloat jacket, a coat which provides buoyancy and helps retain body heat. The Canadian government named the UVic Thermofloat jacket one of the country's 10 best-designed products in 1978. The Sea Seat, an orally-inflated miniature life raft that holds 180 kilograms, or two large people, can increase predicted survival time to 24 hours, adequate time for rescue in most instances.

Hypothermia is slowly becoming a household word in North America. But in spite of exhaustive research the widespread ignorance concerning this insidious assassin of outdoors enthusiasts remains clearly evident. Coroner's juries continue to rule "death by drowning" when all indications point toward hypothermia as the killer in many cases. Even more disturbing is the inane it-can't-happen-to-me attitude: hypothermia kills dozens of people every year. It can happen to anyone.

CANOES, KAYAKS AND SMALL BOATS ON PACIFIC RIM SEAS

The open seas around Pacific Rim can be treacherous territory for small boats but there are numerous sheltered inlets, bays and channels protected from ocean swells and high winds. Many of the most popular canoeing and kayaking waters, particularly the Broken Group Islands of Barkley Sound, are described in detail in following chapters.

All boaters in the Pacific Rim area should carry equipment required by law. For boats up to 5.5 metres long this includes an approved life jacket for each person, two oars with oarlocks or two paddles, a hand-held bailer or manual pump and some type of sound signalling device. Other equipment that may be handy but is not required by law includes a sponge to mop up water, a spare paddle, wet-weather clothing, drinking water, a pocket knife and matches in a waterproof container.

It's unwise to travel Pacific Rim waters without a compass and hydrographic charts. Tide tables for Tofino, which apply to the entire Pacific Rim area, are also needed. Details on how to acquire charts and tide tables, along with information on boating hazards are given in the following chapters, in the paddling and fishing sections on specific areas.

Kayaking near Benson Island

PACIFIC RIM FISHING — ISLANDS, INLETS AND OPEN SEAS

Sport fishing is big business at Pacific Rim, particularly in Barkley Sound. By the mid-1980s salmon fishing out of Ucluelet and Bamfield, on opposite sides of the sound, was rapidly forming the basis of a sizable tourist industry and new motels and lodges were being built to cater to sport fishermen. Some rent boats and equipment, with or without guides. Some offer fishing packages including accommodation, guides, boats and other amenities. There is also good fishing out of Tofino where similar facilities for anglers are available. Information on charters, boat rentals, accommodation and camping, and other facilities for fishermen is available from local tourist bureaus.

Anglers who fish the waters of Pacific Rim should be aware of the hazards and be equipped to deal with rough seas. Except in sheltered waters, such as in the Broken Group Islands, cartop boats are too small and anything under five metres could be risky. Fog is a summer hazard to all boaters. To fish Pacific Rim you need tide tables for Tofino, a compass and hydrographic charts. Federal saltwater licences are required to fish salmon and bottomfish, and regulations are usually available where licences can be purchased. Fisheries officers regularly patrol Barkley Sound and Parks Canada wardens are empowered to enforce certain fishing regulations in Pacific Rim Park.

Details concerning sales of charts, tide tables, licences, types of fish, best places and times to fish and other needs of fishermen are provided in each chapter.

While many Pacific Rim salmon fishermen arrive heavily equipped in high-speed power boats, canoeists, kayakers and small boat owners may carry minimal gear for fishing calm waters. People paddling the waters off Tofino or in the Broken Group Islands during summer are wise to troll a bucktail fly or lightly-weighted Kripple K spoon as they travel from point to point. Only about 15 metres of line is needed to snare a big chinook and if cohoes are in the neighborhood you could take them on the surface 5 or 10 metres behind the boat.

The following information on reading the water and drift fishing could be helpful to people fishing from small boats with light gear. It's based partially on the author's own experience, mainly on advice from some of B.C.'s most experienced salmon anglers.

Reading the Water — Watch Fish, Not Fishermen

The angler who dangles his lure over the gunwale and hopes for a strike usually gets skunked. The one who reads the water

17

and fishes the likely spots lands the lunkers.

The days of hit-and-miss salmon fishing are no longer afford-able. Without investing sizable sums for basic gear you can't even play the game, and with additional costs for boats, bait and bever-age, who can afford to lose? The winners are those who under-stand something of the elusive salmon's habits, the fishermen who learn to read the water before dropping their tackle over the side.

Reading the water, for some anglers, is glancing around the bay for the greatest concentration of boats and heading over to get in on the action. Tight little groups of boats that gather off points or rocks often begin as one or two boats with no fish and prolifer-ate to a sizable fleet, with no fish. The highliners, meanwhile, may be sitting in a back eddy, filling their boats with salmon. They fol-low the fish, not the fishermen.

The most convenient clue to the whereabouts of salmon is surface activity — seabirds and baitfish. Gulls and terns have a habit of noisily advertising their success in locating schools of minnows, particularly when great numbers of herring "ball up" in an effort to escape the jaws of hungry salmon and seabirds. Anglers have been known to drop a buzz bomb or pirken into a herring ball, get a good strike, and reel in a glaucous-winged gull.

Birds feeding on the surface indicate schools of baitfish within the top four or five metres. Occasionally baitfish will jump en masse or swim right on the surface, giving a momentary impres-sion of raindrops hitting the water.

If there are diving birds — murres or cormorants — feeding with gulls or terns, chances are the fish may be deeper, about 10 or 15 metres. If only diving birds are around, the fish could be as deep as 30 metres.

Finding salmon is more difficult without the help of seabirds but tide tables and hydrographic charts provide some useful clues. Fish, like people, prefer the path of least resistance so they rarely linger in the strongest currents. When the tide is running, salmon are likely to be lying on the bottom where the current is slowest. At slack tide they move closer to the surface, especially during periods of low light such as dawn or dusk. Besides telling you the depth, and time of slack tide, charts and tide tables can help you locate back eddies where baitfish and salmon often con-gregate.

Flood tides and ebb tides flow in opposite directions and back eddies form on the same side of a point, reef or island as the tidal direction. If, for example, the tide is ebbing to the north, the back eddy would be on the north side of a point. On the flood tide the back eddy would form on the opposite or south side of the point. The same principles apply to vertical back eddies, which form near reefs or underwater ledges. Find a reef on your chart and if the tide is ebbing to the north, fish the north side of the reef. If you catch a fish you'll probably want to return to that spot, but don't make the mistake of disregarding the tides. If you fish there on a flood tide next trip, the fish will be on the opposite side of the reef. Tidelines are often visible on the surface where currents meet. Ripples or rips alongside glass-smooth water, or long streams of bubbles and weed, show where currents meet. As in back eddies, fish are likely to be where the current is weakest, along the edge of the tideline rather than in the middle.

There is no guaranteed method or place to catch salmon: everyone gets skunked at times, regardless of expertise. Sometimes the fish just aren't around. Fishing is a fine science and, as all fine scientists know, only a combination of factors working together brings success.

Drift Fishing — Maximum Sport from Minimum Gear

Old fishermen never die, they say, but old fishing methods do and a growing number of west coast fishermen are chucking their heavy trolling rigs in favor of light, drift fishing tackle. Drift fishing, a technique pioneered in Vancouver Island waters, is a back-to-basics way of fishing that gives maximum sport from minimum gear. Not to be confused with drifting rivers for steelhead or trout, drift fishing is precisely what the name implies — fishing from a drifting boat without the objectionable noise and foul fumes of an outboard motor. With light rods and reels and a few weighted lures, drift fishermen working within 10 metres of the surface are finding they can consistently outfish traditional deep-water trollers under the right conditions.

Drift fishing is patterned after simple cod jigging and although some of the lures are similar to a few used by Scandinavian fishermen, it is a method not widely practised outside the British Columbia coast. Local sport fishermen have modified various lures and refined the technique through trial and error.

The equipment is simple: a light, soft-tipped rod about 2.5 metres to 3 metres long, a single-action or spinning reel, a couple of hundred metres of 15 or 20-pound test line, and half a dozen lures. The buzz bomb, created on Vancouver Island, is probably the best known and oldest drift fishing lure. Others, such as the stingsilda, deadly dick or pirken, are equally successful.

The methods of fishing all of these lures are basically the same but the action produced by each differs with the shape and bend of the lure. A buzz bomb, for example, flutters in a spinning motion as it sinks, while a pirken falls more like an oak leaf, at irregular angles. The purpose of the lure is to imitate a crippled bait-fish such as a sandlance, anchovy or herring minnow, and attract big spring and coho salmon feeding in and below the schools of baitfish.

Drift fishing in Pacific Rim waters is best in early spring and summer when chinooks feed on spawning sandlance in shallow waters, usually less than 30 metres deep. The salmon feed near a sandy bottom and the lure should be worked within a few centimetres of the seabed. In late June and July, herring minnows averaging about seven or eight centimetres in length move into shallow bays and hang around anywhere from the surface down to 10 metres.

Chinook salmon follow the minnows into shore and feed. Some anglers believe small chinooks feed in the middle of the minnow schools while the big monsters mill around below, gobbling crippled minnows missed by the feeders above. The real action starts in late summer and fall when mature coho salmon begin to mix with the chinooks as they move toward rivers to spawn. Although cohoes are generally smaller than chinooks, they are frantic feeders and offer more fun per pound than the silver chinooks.

Landing a Pacific salmon

There is disagreement among expert anglers about the importance of color in a lure. While it is advisable to use a lure of color similar to the bait, it is probably more important to imitate the size of the bait. A lure the same size or slightly larger than the baitfish will likely produce the best results.

When you have selected a spot, tie a one-metre leader to the lure and join it to the line with a swivel. The swivel will prevent the line from twisting as the lure turns in the water. Start within three metres of the surface, gently lifting the rod and then letting the line slacken and the lure sink. The salmon will usually hit as the lure falls and the strike may not be immediately apparent. Be careful not to jerk the rod on the upward motion as the hook could get yanked from the salmon's mouth.

If there is no action near the surface drop the lure another metre or two, always keeping track of the amount of line you let out so you can duplicate the depth once you have found the fish.

There are times when the water appears to be boiling with life. Baitfish glitter within inches of the surface and squawking gulls and terns swoop down to pluck minnows from the sea, hardly making a splash. This is the time for spin casting. Using the same type of lure, cast into the minnow schools and retrieve the lure slowly, pulling the rod tip up and letting the lure drop every few seconds. When a fish hits, give the rod a tug and set the hook. Keep the line taut but set the drag on the reel to let the fish run. A good-sized chinook or coho may take off a dozen times before it is tired enough to net.

The advantages of drift fishing are obvious. It saves energy and allows the fisherman to enjoy the serenity of dawn or dusk on the sea. It is a highly productive method which can be done from rowboats, canoes, kayaks, docks or rocks and it's simple enough for anyone, regardless of age or experience.

Shellfish Collectors Beware of Red Tides

In 1943 the federal government established a program to monitor the toxicity of shellfish caused by red tides. This deadly phenomenon is caused by microscopic, single-celled algae that produce some of the most potent natural poisons in the world. Filter-feeding shellfish, such as mussels, oysters or clams, are insensitive to the poisons and accumulate them in their digestive glands. People and other warm-blooded animals, however, can die from ingesting the poisons.

As these algae drift about in surface waters, utilizing sunlight for growth, they go through annual cycles and multiply many times. A "bloom" occurs each year for about two or three weeks and wind and current conditions often force the algae to concentrate in small areas. Many of these tiny organisms are a reddish color and when they concentrate they may give the ocean a tomato-soup appearance.

When these algae are consumed by shellfish the phenomenon is known as paralytic shellfish poisoning because the toxins, when consumed by people and other animals, inhibit the transmission of nerve impulses, causing muscular paralysis and possible death by asphyxiation. People who eat contaminated shellfish may feel a tingling in their lips and tongue, their fingertips and toes may become numb and finally they'll lose muscle control. Vomiting should be induced and a doctor should be called.

Under the federal government's monitoring program, weekly samples are collected from shellfish and tested. If toxicity levels exceed certain limits the shellfish area is closed to harvesting and signs are posted nearby to warn people. Some bans remain in effect for several months, even years, and it is both illegal and dangerous to disregard them. Several areas at Pacific Rim are frequently closed to shellfish harvesting due to paralytic shellfish poisoning. The Broken Group Islands are almost always closed. Check for signs or with fisheries officers before collecting shellfish.

Many waters are not affected by red tides and shellfish can be collected without federal fishing licences. Mussels, oysters or clams taken from uncontaminated areas make great meals cooked by campfire. Crabs, shrimp and other shellfish that are not filter-feeders are not affected by red tides. There are legal limits for all shellfish harvesting and fishing regulations should be checked before you head to the beach in search of seashore delicacies.

GRAVEYARD OF THE PACIFIC — A SHIPWRECK HUNTER'S HAVEN

Hundreds of ships have met their doom along the storm-torn shores of Pacific Rim between Hot Springs Cove and Port Renfrew. It can be a wretched place in winter, with wicked winds and enormous seas that can drag a disabled ship into reef-ridden shores and smash it to pieces within hours. The most ominous shores are between Port Renfew and Cape Beale, an area generally known as the Graveyard of the Pacific.

It seems paradoxical that the Spanish explorer Balboa named this ocean the Pacific because of the tranquility he saw when he discovered it in 1513. But today, as in Balboa's day, the Pacific ocean is often as calm as a millpond at dawn. These peaceful periods may last for days before fresh frontal systems sweep in from the open sea.

A few of the shipwrecks which now lie in the more sheltered waters of Pacific Rim have become major attractions for scuba divers, underwater maritime museums with a host of artifacts to be salvaged or left untouched forever on the ocean floor. Some have been officially declared historic sites, a designation which gives them legal protection from overzealous treasure hunters. All wrecks within Pacific Rim National Park are also protected by law.

Charter boat operators in Tofino, Ucluelet and Bamfield who offer diving trips in the waters off Tofino and in Barkley Sound are usually familiar with the history and locations of the area's shipwrecks. They also know where to find some of the prolific marine life that has earned the coastal waters of British Columbia a well-known reputation as one of the finest scuba diving territories in the world. Anemones, enormous barnacles, sponges, abalone, urchins and sea stars blanket the bottom of the sea. Divers swim through jungles of kelp, nurseries for herring and a variety of fish. There are underwater galleries, reefs and caves, some inhabited by timid octopi or wolf eels. Visibility in winter is excellent and most of the scenery is within 20 metres of the surface. Air is available and divers who prefer to dive without guides can rent boats. Information on Pacific Rim diving and charters is available from local tourist centres.

The shipwrecks of Pacific Rim are too deep for divers without scuba gear but lowly snorkellers can enjoy much of the colorful underwater scenery around shallow shores and reefs. Thick-skinned snorkellers may swim without wet suits in Barkley Sound during summer, but those with wet suits can endure the cold longer and dive year-round. Moonsnails, urchins, sea stars and anemones, rockfish, flounders, rock crabs, Dungeness, perch and an array of marine plants are common within the top five metres of water.

Anyone with the common sense not to snorkel amid entangling kelp beds, or where currents are strong, can dive safely in Pacific Rim waters. Unlike scuba divers, who are limited by air supplies, snorkellers can stay in the water as long as they like, or make two or three dives in a day without buying air. It's a simple, fascinating sport, practised in pretty places. It can be habit-forming.

PACIFIC RIM HUNTING — MAINLY WATERFOWL

The area around Tofino is well known among Vancouver Island waterfowl hunters. Canada geese and a variety of ducks are taken from mid-fall to early winter. Federal migratory bird permits are needed and can be picked up from post offices in Tofino, Ucluelet and Port Alberni.

Blacktail deer are often hunted throughout much of the Pacific Rim area by local sportsmen. Nonresidents with guides frequently come to Pacific Rim for black bears. All hunters need provincial hunting licences, which can be purchased from government agents' offices in Port Alberni and Ucluelet and from local sporting goods stores.

Species tags and regulations are usually available from sporting goods stores. Certain shooting restrictions are imposed within municipal boundaries and all of Pacific Rim Park is a no-shooting area. Check the regulations.

PACIFIC RIM WILDLIFE — WHALES TO PERIWINKLES

The wild animals of Pacific Rim are as varied as the habitats they occupy. There are bears and cougars in the forests, seabirds and sea lions on offshore rocks, mice and ruffed grouse in the fields, mussels, chitons, limpets and periwinkles in the tide pools, and great blue herons, migrating swans and thousands of wintering waterfowl on the mudflats near Grice Bay and Tofino.

The most obvious wildlife are the birds, from stately bald eagles and clumsy cormorants to tiny kinglets and chickadees. Pacific Rim is on the western edge of the Pacific flyway and more than a million migratory birds grace the spring and autumn skies on their annual journeys. Hundreds of gulls may cluster at the sea edge, laying tracks in the wet sand. More than 250 bird species occur in Pacific Rim Park: about 65 stay year-round and over 50 breed here.

More than 2,000 seabirds nest in about half a dozen colonies between the south end of Ucluth Peninsula and Cox Point. Most abundant are glaucous-winged gulls — about 100 nest on White Island in Schooner Cove, 280 may breed on Sea Lion Rocks and more than 800 nest on Florencia Islet. The same three colonies support a breeding population of about 200 pelagic cormorants. Farther north, near the entrance to Clayoquot Sound, more than 14,000 birds nest on Plover Reefs and Cleland Island, an eight-hectare ecological reserve. They include 10,000 Leach's storm petrels, 3,000 glaucous-winged gulls, 1,000 rhinocerous auklets, 200 pigeon guillemots and a few dozen fork-tailed storm petrels, Cassin's auklets, common murres, tufted puffins and black oystercatchers.

South of Long Beach, in the island-studded waters of Barkley Sound, nearly 2,000 seabirds nest between Amphitrite Point and

Cape Beale. Starlight Reef, about six kilometres southeast of Amphitrite Point near the entrance to Loudoun Channel, is a nesting ground for more than 130 Brandt's cormorants and 600 glaucous-winged gulls. A similar number of glaucous-winged gulls nest farther up the channel on Great Bear Rocks. On the opposite side of Barkley Sound, at the north end of Imperial Eagle Channel, is a 53-hectare ecological reserve to protect the nesting birds at Baeria Rocks. It's used by more than 400 glaucous-winged gulls and 60 pelagic cormorants.

Nesting cormorants

Although there are fewer nesting areas along the West Coast Trail, one colony has at least seven species. Seabird Rocks, near Pachena Bay, is a nesting site for 1,000 Leach's storm petrels, 800 glaucous-winged gulls, 300 rhinocerous auklets, 200 Cassin's auklets, 100 pigeon guillemots, 40 tufted puffins and 20 fork-tailed storm petrels.

One particularly interesting Pacific Rim breeder is the black oystercatcher, a goofy-looking crow-sized bird with a long, bright orange bill. Its title is a misnomer because it has never been known to catch oysters. It uses its bill to open mussels by severing the adductor muscle. You can see them probing tide pools, "peeping" angrily at intruders. Flocks of between 50 and 70 are common on the south end of Vancouver Island during winter. Other long-billed shorebirds are dowitchers, sandpipers, yellowlegs, godwits, dunlins, snipes and whimbrels.

Grice Bay, a part of Pacific Rim Park, and the mudflats near the village of Tofino are a bird watcher's haven. They're an important stopover for thousands of migrating waterfowl. From October to December as many as 3,000 Canada geese may be on the flats and up to 500 may winter through January to March. In midwinter 50 or 75 trumpeter swans, part of Vancouver Island's wintering population of about 2,000, are often seen in the Tofino area.

Winter in the inlet may see 8,000 dabbling ducks — mallards, widgeon, pintails, teal and others — while another 8,000-odd diving ducks such as scaups, goldeneyes, buffleheads, mergansers and scoters share the same waters. Four loon species frequent these waters, two of which — the common and red-throated loon — are known to breed in the Pacific Rim area. The throaty croak of the great blue heron often startles unsuspecting bird watchers. These spindle-legged, stork-like birds spend their days wading the shallows in search of seashore delicacies, standing motionless until an unwary victim swims within striking distance.

A 2.2-kilometre road near the north end of the park leads to Grice Bay where there are picnic tables and a paved boat-launching ramp. Pacific Rim naturalists can offer advice about canoe trips in these sheltered waters: take your own boat or ask the information staff where to rent one.

Of all the birds at Pacific Rim the most awe-inspiring is unquestionably the bald eagle, the lordly master of the sky. Pacific Rim is the only national park in Canada where bald eagles can be seen daily throughout the year. While early-rising campers at Long Beach may see eagles in summer, these statuesque birds are more plentiful in fall and winter when fewer people are around. For a detailed look at bald eagles see p. 31 .

The raucous chatter of the Steller's jay is an attention grabber. These robin-sized, iridescent blue freebooters shamelessly pilfer unguarded food at picnic tables and campgrounds. They're as fearless as they are curious and the moment a camper's back is turned they zip down to make the heist. Other camp robbers — ravens, crows and red squirrels — are more cautious, usually waiting until a campsite is deserted before beginning their thievery.

Campers should also beware of racoons. They prowl around at night, overturning anything that smells of food. They're interesting to watch but can be aggressive if cornered or if you try to retrieve their loot. Beach campers should be more concerned with mice and mink. Mice scamper out of the uplands and across the beaches at night, searching through garbage, food bags or unwashed dishes. They can easily gnaw through a new backpack to get at food inside. Their scratching is an irritating sound to someone trying to sleep through a robbery. Mink, slinky brown cousins of the weasel, are more discreet about their thefts but they often hide under upturned boats and boxes, leaving foul-smelling droppings within whiffing distance of campsites. If possible, lock your food in a car or hang it out of reach. People who sleep on the beach under the stars may find the lowly sand flea a nuisance. They're marine crustaceans that jump around the beaches at night in search of food. The little hoppers jump onto sleeping bags or tarps, often landing on your face or leaping into the sack with you. If you awake to the sound of rain drops, but find the sky is a mass of stars, you're being attacked by a battalion of bothersome sand fleas. Fortunately they don't seem to bite.

Improperly stored food may attract black bears, fascinating animals to watch from a distance, but rather unwelcome visitors to your tent. They're not cuddly, endearing honey-lovers that chase butterflies and crave the affectionate touch of the human hand, as some movie-makers would have us believe. A bear, hundreds of kilos of strength and agility, is an easily frightened, dangerously unpredictable animal, defensive when threatened, savage when angered.

There are no grizzly bears on Vancouver Island but estimates from the early 1980s suggest there are probably between 5,000 and 12,000 black bears. Although attacks are infrequent, some that do occur could be avoided. To discourage bears from wandering into your campsite, be sure to cook your meals outside the tent: smells which linger long after dinner can attract a hungry bear from a great distance. Food should be kept in vehicles when possible or suspended in a tree.

Park wardens are occasionally called to Long Beach to trap bears which have been bothering campers or hikers. In spite of their size and strength, black bears are timid beasts and would prefer to avoid encounters with people. Huge mounds of bear dung, steaming with warmth and freshness, occasionally embellish boardwalks and trails when there is no other sign of a bear. Unfortunate experiences with bears can often be avoided by making the animal aware of your presence. Shouting, ringing bells or rattling a tin of stones are effective except in dense brush or near rushing water. Food sources, like berry patches or carcasses, should be avoided and dogs, which can enrage bears, are best left at home. Bears have poor eyesight: one standing erect is normally more curious than aggressive, merely getting a better whiff to determine who's in its territory.

There are no guaranteed life-saving methods to follow when confronted by a bear, but some behavior has proven successful. Always leave a bear an escape route. If a black bear is seen from a distance, make a wide detour. If you meet one on a trail, speak softly and back slowly toward a tree, removing your pack to distract it. Climb as high as you can but remember that black bears can also climb trees. If there's no escape, play dead. Drop to the ground face down, lift your legs up to your chest, clasp your hands over the back of your neck and hope for the best. Wearing your pack could help shield your body.

Other large mammals to inhabit the Pacific Rim area are cougars and timber wolves. Both are seen rarely although wolves have been known to wander onto the beaches at Long Beach. There has been a small number of wolf attacks on people in recent years on Vancouver Island's north end, but before that, wolf attacks were unheard of. Wolf numbers on Vancouver Island appear to change more drastically than other large predators and estimates vary from 200 to 1,500 animals. Wolf and cougar populations fluctuate with the availability of prey. There are probably about 1,200 cougars on Vancouver Island, feeding mainly on blacktail deer. Cougar attacks on people are rare, usually inflicted by sick or injured animals. Two occurred in the Pacific Rim area in 1985. The most common sightings of wolves and cougars are invariably the animal's hind end disappearing into the bush.

Blacktail deer are also elusive forest dwellers but are seen more often than any of the large predators. Their distinctive cloven-hoofed tracks can be found near fresh water sources and on beaches. A big buck may weigh as much as 110 kilograms. These deer may swim from one island to another in the Broken Group.

The most visible large mammals in the Pacific Rim area are the sea lions. Two species — California and Steller's sea lions — inhabit the Pacific Rim area. These bulky beasts roam the coast, hauling out at specific sites. Hundreds may arrive at a haulout, stay a few days or weeks, then move on, while smaller numbers may remain through winter or summer. They occupy several haulouts along the Pacific Rim shoreline from Plover Reefs in the northwest to Carmanah Point in the southeast. They're often seen ploughing along the shore and swimming into sheltered inlets in search of herring and salmon. A detailed look at these fascinating beasts, with information on where to find them at Pacific Rim, is provided on p. 35 .

Even larger than the Steller's sea lion is the elephant seal, a grayish-brown beast with a long, wrinkled, inflatable snout. Big bulls may measure up to four metres long and weigh 2.5 tonnes. These whoppers are seen occasionally in Barkley Sound.

Harbor seals, smaller cousins of the sea lion, are found nearly everywhere along the B.C. coast. They bob about in the waves off Long Beach and forage for fish in the sheltered waters of Tofino, Ucluelet and Bamfield inlets and amid the islands of Barkley Sound. They haul their cigar-shaped bodies out on rocky shores and offshore islets and wallow in the sun. Unlike Steller's sea lions, which breed at only three rookeries in northern B.C., harbor seals bear their pups on beaches all along the coast. They're cautious but curious and have a habit of following canoeists and kayakers around sheltered harbors. If you see a shiny, spotted head with a pointed, whiskery nose and bulging eyes slinking quietly along the surface, you're looking at a harbor seal.

Some of the same protected waters are used by the river otter, a member of the weasel family. It shouldn't be confused with a much larger member of the weasel family, the sea otter, a marine mammal which, in Canada, inhabits only isolated areas on the northwest coast of Vancouver Island. Sea otters once inhabited most of Vancouver Island's western shores but were wiped out by avaricious 18th and 19th-century fur traders. They were successfully reintroduced from Alaska during the late 1960s and early 1970s. River otters are common along Pacific Rim shores, where families of four or five are often spotted climbing onto docks or swimming between moored boats.

The largest marine animals at Pacific Rim, of course, are the whales. The annual migration of the Pacific gray whale, described in detail on p. 61 , is a spectacular event which draws people from around the world to Long Beach. Between late February and May an estimated 17,000 of these magnificent mammals thunder past Long Beach within viewing distance of shore. About 40 remain around Pacific Rim Park throughout summer and are being seen with increasing frequency by people canoeing the Broken Group Islands and hiking the West Coast Trail.

Other whales, such as the humpback, finback, sei, and minke are occasionally sighted off Pacific Rim shores. One of the few to enter narrow inlets and bays is the killer whale, the sea lion's most formidable foe. This aquatic carnivore is known to chase seals and sea lions right up onto beaches. It also eats seabirds, porpoises, salmon, squid and occasionally attacks larger whales.

The tall, black dorsal fins of killer whales breaking the surface is an exciting sight. More often than not, they travel in pods, or families, and three or four may surface simultaneously. It's difficult for terrestrial beings like ourselves to imagine these immense beasts roaming the sea around us, traveling in closely knit families, communicating among themselves over great distances. Once you have seen them at close range, close enough to hear that unmistakable rush of air firing from their lungs, you will always watch for them again.

Once considered a nuisance by fishermen and mariners, the killer whale, or orca, has aroused the curiosity of scientists and earned long-overdue respect for its apparent intelligence and mysterious communicative abilities. They are toothed whales,

29

bulls measuring up to eight metres long, cows about six. The dorsal fin of a male may be as high as two metres. The total number of killer whales patrolling the B.C. coast is only about 300.

Pacific Rim not only has the world's largest animals; some of the smallest inhabit the intertidal zone. They're most prolific in sheltered coves, protected from shifting sands and breakers. At low tides the pools along rocky shores become outdoor aquariums, teeming with minute creatures from sculpins to limpets. In a single glance you could see periwinkles, hermit crabs, barnacles, mussels, chitons, anemones, urchins, snails and sea stars.

Exploring tide pools

Sculpin fishing is a popular sport at tide pools. With a bit of practice these horny-headed fish can be scooped up with a plastic cup or jar, or even by small hands. They're fast but vulnerable within the confines of a tide pool and they don't seem to mind living in a bucket for a few minutes while everyone has a closer look. Change the water frequently and don't keep them out of their natural environment for too long. Handle all marine life gently and never use sticks to poke about in tide pools.

Tide pools are among the stops by park naturalists on their rounds in Pacific Rim Park. For more information on park naturalist services and programs see p. 60 .

The prolific marine life of Pacific Rim is the mainstay of several charter boat operations based in Tofino, Ucluelet and Bamfield. Tours of seabird colonies and sea lion haulouts, whale-watching excursions, fishing and scuba charters and general nature trips are an exciting way to take a closer look at Pacific Rim's natural heritage. Pacific Rim Airlines offers short sightseeing flights out of Tofino. For information on commercial nature tours contact the Pacific Rim Park information centre or tourist bureaus in Ucluelet, Tofino and Bamfield.

BALD EAGLES — FROM BOUNTIES TO BOUNTIFUL

Most of the bald eagles around Pacific Rim are in Barkley Sound where the Broken Islands provide extensive shoreline for them to forage. Surveys in the early 1970s indicate the eagle concentrations in Barkley Sound may be the highest in the province. At least 100 pairs nest in the Pacific Rim area. There are at least 26 nests on Meares Island near Tofino.

There's a certain nobility to birds of prey: to see an eagle soaring over the trees is rewarding, but to watch a bald eagle hunt is a rare privilege. From the top of a snag tree the eagle selects its prey, possibly a coot or a duck from a flock floating on a lagoon. One ill-fated straggler is singled out and the great white-headed predator lunges, forcing its prey to dive. The bird surfaces and the eagle strikes, scarcely allowing time for a breath of air. The bird dives, surfaces, and the eagle persists, again and again until its quarry is too exhausted to seek refuge in the depths of the lagoon. The attack is over in moments. The eagle unceremoniously snatches its enfeebled victim from the water and leaves as quickly, as quietly, as it came.

The bald eagle's unparalleled hunting skills are a paradox, the cause of both its salvation and its demise. Possibly the most versatile predator in Canada and probably the most resourceful bird of prey on the continent, the bald eagle, like the golden eagle which inhabits British Columbia in smaller numbers, was among the most persecuted raptors in North America until the early 1960s, when new laws declared it a protected species. Although the bald eagle is the emblem of the United States, Americans and Canadians alike considered this heraldic bird vermin, a sheep and poultry killer for which a government-sponsored bounty was offered as a means of exterminating it. It is believed today that the number of bald eagles which survive outside B.C. and Alaska is smaller than the total number killed in Alaska in the days when the carnage was encouraged.

Bald eagle

Despite the senseless extermination efforts of former generations, bald eagles remain plentiful on the north Pacific coast. It is
estimated that between 16,000 and 20,000 adult eagles inhabit
B.C., particularly along the jagged, forested coast, and substantially more thrive on the coastal waterways of Alaska. There is no
indication that their numbers are dwindling and in some areas
their populations appear to be growing. This stately predator, one
of 34 raptorial bird species in B.C., has an immense range, spread-
ing from Labrador across the continent and south to Florida and
Mexico, but their numbers are extremely limited outside the
North Pacific. Nearly all of the bald eagles in the world live in
British Columbia and Alaska.

The bald eagle is associated almost exclusively with large
bodies of water and though some inhabit inland lakes and rivers,
it is primarily a maritime bird, relying on the prolific seabird and
marine life of the coast as its major food source. Autumn and early
winter salmon runs are particularly attractive to eagles and hundreds congregate along B.C. rivers to feed on fish carcasses, a habit
which has unjustly earned these birds a reputation as scavengers.

Eagles are seafood gourmets, proficient fishermen and hunters that stalk rocky shorelines and beaches, probing seaweed and
poking in tidal pools for shellfish and crabs. Biologists who
climbed into an eagle nest in the Queen Charlotte Islands were
surprised to find 357 abalone shells. It is not uncommon to see an
eagle swoop from a shore-side branch and clench an unwary fish
swimming near the surface. If small fish such as herring or minnows are plentiful, an eagle can devour one in mid-flight before
diving in for another catch. Larger fish, up to three kilograms,
which unwisely swim near the surface are also fair game. The
eagle circles overhead until a fish is sighted, then descends and
sinks its talons into the flesh. Unable to return to flight, the eagle
uses its wings to swim ashore with the fish in tow. Occasionally
eagles drown trying to make shore.

While the eagle's reputation as a scavenger may be unjust, it
is well known as a pirate. In many cases the loser is a hard-work-
ing osprey, an equally proficient fisherman but a reluctant defen-
der of its catch against a determined eagle. The eagle's aerial agility allows it to closely pursue every twist and turn until the osprey
sees its escape attempts are hopeless. The eagle, with its 2.2-metre
wingspan, chases the osprey in flight, forcing it to drop its catch
for the eagle to retrieve. It is with similar deftness that the eagle
preys upon loons, seagulls, coots, ducks and storm petrels.

As intriguing as the eagle's hunting methods are its nesting
habits. Partners for life, each pair returns to the same nest year
after year, to lay the eggs and share incubation duties. Only fully-
mature five-year-olds, with distinctive white heads and tails, pair

up to breed. A mature bird may measure almost a metre from its tail to its head and weigh between 3.5 and 6.3 kilograms, the female being one-third larger than its mate.

Huge stick nests, which when first built usually measure about a metre across by 60 centimetres deep, are constructed within the crown of mature conifers. Occasionally nests are made on cliffs and there have been instances where nests were discovered on the ground in coastal forests. The inside of the nests are lined with soft materials, such as seaweed or grasses, and each year about 20 kilograms of material are added. Nests weighing a tonne are common. One nest found in an old cedar tree on Bonilla Island, on the north coast of B.C., measured 6.6 metres across and 4.8 metres deep. It was impossible to estimate its weight but researchers believed it was at least half a century old. It eventually toppled out of the tree, as many nests do.

Nesting eagles are sensitive to human disturbances but will tolerate the presence of people if they do not appear to pose a threat. Surveys have shown, however, that eagles will abandon their eggs if a person climbs into the nest. If the nest is invaded after the eggs have hatched, the adults will remain with the young but will not return the following year. Different types of aircraft appear to have inexplicable effects on behavior during nesting season. If fixed-wing aircraft are used to survey nests the birds don't seem to mind, but if a helicopter is used the birds will finish the nesting cycle for the year but abandon the nest the next year.

It was once thought that bald eagles traveled only short distances throughout the year but studies now have shown they are migratory. Migrations begin after the young have fledged and usually by September or October the nests are deserted. The distances some eagles travel are astounding when one considers they were believed to be a nonmigratory bird. Two eagles banded in the Chilkat River area of Alaska during late fall were found on Vancouver Island in late winter. In another survey, eagles wearing radio transmitters and banded in Washington's Skagit Valley were later located on the Queen Charlotte Islands.

Eagle watching is an intriguing pastime and the best times are during B.C.'s salmon runs. From November to March eagles are plentiful nearly anywhere that fish are plentiful. After March, when nesting begins, the simplest way to locate eagles is to travel about 200 metres offshore in a boat. Boats can be rented or you can take a nature cruise in a charter boat. Using a telescope or binoculars, look for "eagle trees," tall snags which for some unknown reason are favorite perches for bald eagles. If you spot an individual eagle, scan the tallest nearby trees from about halfway up, to the top, for the nest or the mate.

While bald eagles are not unique to Pacific Rim, their scarcity in other parts of the world gives them a special place among the wildlife of British Columbia. Persecuted and misunderstood for decades, bald eagles only recently have become a predator to admire, to study and to protect. It seems the more we learn about them, the more fascinating they become.

PACIFIC RIM SEA LIONS EASY TO SEE

Both Steller's and California sea lions roam the coast of Pacific Rim, hauling out at specific sites, some of which can easily be seen from shore. Most common is the auburn-colored Steller's, although the smaller, darker California sea lion is appearing in growing numbers. A full-grown Steller's bull is a tonne of blubber and fur, twice the size of the largest grizzly bear, yet it moves with a speed and agility that belies its bulky form. Out of the water the sea lion appears sluggish, propped up awkwardly on its fore-flippers, mindful of its vulnerability to terrestrial creatures like man. But in the oceans of British Columbia it swims gracefully throughout its domain, fearing only the killer whale.

At Pacific Rim hundreds may arrive at a haulout, stay a few weeks or a month, burping and barking, then move on, while smaller numbers may remain through winter or summer. They occupy one haulout in the Long Beach part of the park — Sea Lion Rocks — and two at opposite ends of Long Beach. Sea Lion Rocks are a year-round haulout, easily visible from Combers Beach or through a telescope mounted on the rocks at Green Point. Since 1913, when the first records were made of Steller's, or northern sea lions, on Sea Lion Rocks, as many as 350 have been counted during winter and 650 have been seen at once between June and August. Big bulls measuring more than three metres long laze in the afternoon sun, seemingly oblivious to the pounding of the seas against the rocks.

Plover Reefs, near the entrance to Clayoquot Sound northwest of Long Beach, are a winter haulout for Steller's sea lions, a pleasant treat for people flying from Tofino to Hot Springs Cove. More than 200 sea lions may winter at Plover Reefs and over 300 have been counted in April.

California sea lions don't often share these particular rocks with the Steller's sea lions but by the mid-1980s large numbers of California sea lions were appearing each winter near Wya Point, the most southerly point in the Long Beach section of the park. They haul out on an islet south of Wya Point, and in 1984 a total of 1,777 were counted one day in February, the highest number of California sea lions ever observed on any Vancouver Island haulout up to that time. The islet is visible from Wya Point, which can

35

be reached by hiking the Willowbrae and Half Moon Bay trails, described in Chapter 2.

Wouwer Island, on the outer edge of the Broken Group, is a major winter haulout. As many as 1,000 sea lions, mainly Californias, line the boulder beaches on the north side of Wouwer and the south side of nearby Batley Island. Some rocks about 500 metres southwest of Wouwer are used by Steller's sea lions in summer. In April of 1985, 500 California sea lions were counted in the Tiny Group, a small cluster of islets in the Broken Group Islands where sea lions hadn't been noticed before.

Wouwer Island sea lions

On the eastern side of Barkley Sound, near the entrance to Imperial Eagle Channel, hundreds of Steller's and California sea lions have been counted on Folger Island in winter. Few Californias use haulouts along the West Coast Trail but Steller's sea lions are seen at Pachena Point during winter. More than 400 or 500 may be counted on some winter days but a normal winter population may be 100 or 150 animals. A small, flat rock off Carmanah Point may be used in both winter and summer by more than 100 Steller's sea lions. People hiking downwind of Carmanah get lots of warning before they reach the point.

Though sea lions in Canada are protected by law they have become the focus of a coastal controversy because some people believe their populations are out of control. Sea lions are predators which innocently hunt a prey valuable to man — herring and salmon — and as more sea lions appear along the B.C. coast, both sport and commercial fishermen renew their call for population controls. It's a case of history repeating itself.

A decade past the turn of the century fishermen along the western Canadian coast complained that the flourishing herds of Steller's sea lions were devouring a healthy share of the annual salmon and herring harvests. Sea lions were of no value, the fishermen argued, so the federal government quelled their complaints in 1913 with the first study of B.C. sea lions. The study concluded the fishermen were right: the only good sea lion was a dead sea lion, so a bounty was offered on their snouts. Fishermen were encouraged to eliminate the competition, to sell the hides and ship the meat to mink farms. But too much heavy equipment was needed to harvest mammals of such prodigious dimensions so few fishermen bothered to try. The bounty also did little to reduce the numbers of Steller's sea lions.

The Department of Marine and Fisheries, as it was known at the time, took charge and ordered its officers to slaughter them on the breeding rookeries. They shot them in their mating territories and surrounding rocks. They shot them at feeding grounds, at haulouts and resting waters. In the late '60s environmentalists rallied against the "control program" and convinced Parliament, in 1970, to protect all marine mammals under the Fisheries Act.

Today, it's believed that Canada's Steller's sea lion population of 5,700-odd animals is about one-third of the total number that historically inhabited the B.C. coast. And fishermen once again have called for a "control program" to even up the competition for the west coast's precious salmon and herring stocks. In keeping with tradition, the federal government responded with a study of western Canada's sea lions.

The study, which began in 1982, will likely surprise sea lion observers, particularly those who claim we are witnessing a population explosion. It appears B.C.'s breeding population of Steller's sea lions, which mate mainly on rookeries on the southern tip of the Queen Charlotte Islands at Cape St. James, and in the Scott Islands off the northwestern tip of Vancouver Island, isn't changing in size from year to year, and there doesn't seem to be any major recovery from the reductions that occurred before they became protected by law.

Forrester Island, about 15 kilometres north of the B.C.-Alaska border, however, is a rookery with about 9,700 Steller's sea lions, a population which has grown from about 100 in the late 1920s. Many of those animals disperse into B.C. waters after the breeding season.

South of B.C., the populations of California sea lions, with their northernmost breeding area in the Channel Islands near San Francisco, are exploding: by the mid-1980s there were an estimated 100,000. The Channel Islands is also the southernmost American breeding area for Steller's sea lions.

In late June and early July, Steller's sea lions return from their wintering grounds to traditional breeding rookeries. In B.C., about 1,200 pups are born each season, just enough to replace the number which die throughout the year, leaving a stable population. Unburdened by newborn offspring, the males disperse from the breeding rocks and many travel down the coast to southern B.C. waters. The females remain within a few hundred kilometres of the breeding grounds throughout the year. Added to the animals that breed in B.C. and winter down the coast are many Steller's sea lions from Forrester Island as well as some that breed in American waters south of B.C. and move up to B.C. for the winter. By the mid-1980s it was estimated the total breeding population of Steller's sea lions between northern California and Prince William Sound in Alaska was more than 15,000.

Many of the Steller's sea lions that breed off San Francisco move up the coast to winter in northern American and southern Canadian waters. Like Steller's, California sea lions disperse from their breeding rookeries and, as their populations increase, a growing number are moving up the coast of North America to spend winter in areas traditionally inhabited mainly by Steller's sea lions. As the California sea lions move toward B.C., Steller's sea lions which once wintered in northern California, Oregon and Washington are being forced into southern B.C. waters. These changes in wintering habits give the impression that B.C.'s breeding population is rapidly increasing when really it is stable: it is the California sea lion populations that are expanding.

The number of California sea lions that intermingle, but don't interbreed, with B.C.'s wintering Steller's sea lions is also growing. By the mid-1980s about 4,500 California sea lions were coming to B.C. for the winter. New haulouts were being established and it's anybody's guess how large the B.C. wintering population of California sea lions will become. Like Steller's sea lions, only California males travel long distances from breeding rookeries at the end of the mating season, leaving the females behind. Until the mid-1970s, sightings of any California sea lions in Canadian waters were rare.

Although these population changes may fluster fishermen they're good news for sea lion observers. The Steller's sea lions that lie on Sea Lion Rocks at Long Beach are visible from shore year-round. The California sea lions near Wya Point can be seen from shore in winter and other sea lions are visible along the West Coast Trail. Local airlines and charter boat operators offer nature cruises to visit sea lion haulouts in the Pacific Rim area and canoeists, kayakers and other boaters can travel out to Steller's sea lions near Wouwer Island.

Wild sea lions are generally not aggressive or timid but they could be unpredictable if spooked. They can usually be approached to within a few metres and noise from outboard motors doesn't appear to bother them. Binoculars, spotting scopes and cameras with telephoto lenses can bring them even closer.

Among the more courageous sea lion observers are scuba divers. Many who swim with sea lions find them extremely curious. They'll swim at high speed directly toward a diver and stop, as if applying brakes, 30 centimetres from the diver's face mask. There are rumors of divers having their regulators torn from their mouths, or having bones broken from charging sea lions, but no confirmed reports from the Pacific Rim area. Swimming among dozens of one-tonne playful sea lions could be dangerous but many divers apparently believe the rewards are worth the risks.

As protected marine mammals, sea lions must not be "caught, killed, disturbed or molested" under the Fisheries Act.

CANADA'S METRIC SYSTEM — SIMPLE AND EFFICIENT

Canada's metric system is often confusing to people unaccustomed to dealing with it but fairly easy to live with once you get used to it. Simple conversions such as inches to centimetres, miles to kilometres, or acres to hectares present little problem when you use the multiplication factors. This book conforms to the metric system.

Here is a simple table to help you understand the metric system:

When you know	Multiply by	To find
centimetres	.4	inches
metres	3.3	feet
kilometres	.63	miles
square metres	1.25	square yards
square kilometres	.4	square miles
hectares	2.5	acres
kilograms	2.2	pounds
Or:		
inches	2.5	centimetres
feet	.3	metres
miles	1.6	kilometres
square yards	.8	square metres
square miles	2.6	square kilometres
acres	.4	hectares
pounds	.45	kilograms

Temperatures are given in celsius and their relationship to the Fahrenheit scale is shown on the following diagram.

Fahrenheit/Celsius

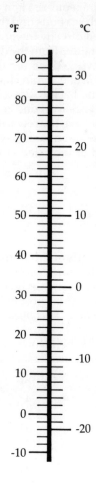

CHAPTER TWO

Long Beach
ENDLESS SAND AND SURF

Anyone who's been to Long Beach knows that bend in the road where you drive over the crest of a hill and are confronted by an endless gray-green stretch of sand and surf, breakers foaming against the shores, tossing plumes of mist above rocks and headlands that stand between the sea and beach. It's the first glimpse of the Pacific Ocean after a meandering drive through the mountains of southern Vancouver Island and it stuns you as you catch it through a clearing in the trees. The vastness is humbling and the beach, strewn with flotsam and driftwood, appears deserted, an invitation to step into the scene and become a part of its rugged beauty.

Before the highway was paved in the early 1970s the only land link between the outside world and Long Beach was a treacherous dirt track from Port Alberni, traveled mainly by the foolishly courageous and hopelessly curious. Even the stalwart inhabitants of Ucluelet and Tofino, the villages at opposite ends of Long Beach, avoided the road when they could. It was a nerve-wracking 110-kilometre crawl over the Mackenzie Range, from sea level at Port Alberni to sea level at Long Beach.

But it was a journey that brought just reward for the discom-

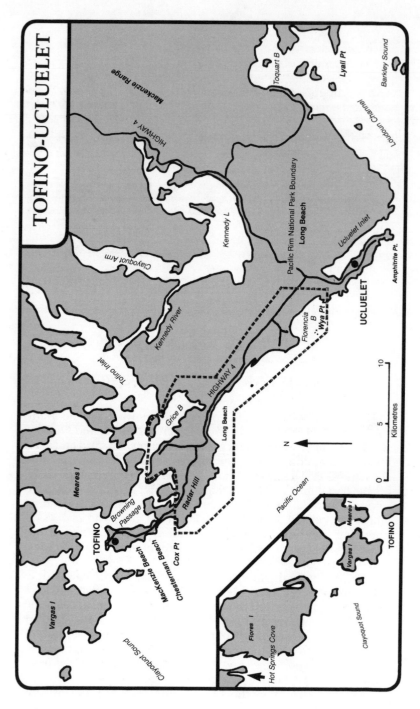

TOFINO-UCLUELET

fort. Many would drive through the night to arrive on the beach just before sunrise. They'd sit barefoot on the logs with their backs to the dawn and watch the breakers rumble in from Japan. For those who saw Long Beach for the first time as the sun climbed behind the mountains, bringing the colors to the sand, the sea, and the forests, many more trips to this special destination would become subconsciously stored in their futures.

Regulations in those days were as scarce as tourists and the beaches between Tofino and Ucluelet became populated by young men and women who'd wandered to the west coast from various parts of the world. During the late 1960s and early '70s Florencia Bay was inhabited by so many that it was included in the 1971 federal census. Sculptors, painters, philosophers, explorers and other vagabonds foraged the beaches for the endless supply of building materials which came ashore with the tides. They built shacks of logs and driftwood, split shakes from wind-fallen cedars; they washed themselves in saunas fashioned from plastic tarps and dried their bodies in fish-net hammocks discarded or lost by passing seine boats. Shanty communities, embellished by cork and glass floats, foreign bottles, bleach jars, shells and other pelagic paraphernalia, became year-round homes for those willing to withstand the winds, the winters and the wilderness. A few even bore their children on the beaches.

Today, with Long Beach a part of Pacific Rim National Park, the squatters have gone. There's an orderliness about the place, an aura of officialism that landed on the beaches with the troops from Parks Canada. They established headquarters on a hill overlooking Wickaninnish Bay and from there the day-to-day affairs of the park are administered. Signs point out specially-designated campgrounds, picnic sites, parking lots and restrooms. An information centre directs visitors to freshly cut trails, meticulously maintained boardwalks and an array of tourist facilities. There are commercial whale-watching cruises, fishing excursions and a growing list of hotels, motels, resorts and lodges. All of this lies at the end of a paved highway that winds through the mountains along the shores of Sproat Lake, through the upper Kennedy River Valley and past Kennedy Lake, the largest body of fresh water on the Island.

The most stubborn nostalgists grumbled about the changes which began at Long Beach in 1971 when Princess Anne officially declared it parkland. Their favorite pioneering place was opened to the masses: they'd be herded with the hordes to campsites someone else had chosen for them. But as the park developed, many realized their selfish worries were unreasonable. If anything, the creation of Pacific Rim National Park has finally preserved a wild and extraordinary coastline, we hope forever, from the industrial endeavors of future generations. The Long Beach section of the park encompasses 81 square kilometres with 30 kilometres of shoreline stretching from Cox Point in the north-west to Wya Point in the south. More than half of the Long Beach shore is sand beach: you can kick off your shoes and hike the beaches and headlands 19 kilometres from Schooner Cove to Half Moon Bay.

Now over half a million people visit Long Beach every year. Nearly 400,000 come between April and October with campers and tents and hopes that the clouds will clear for at least some of their stay. But many come when summer crowds have gone, lured by the pitiless rains and infamous gales that scream in from the open Pacific. They're weather watchers who settle into sea-side cabins to witness the furious winter winds shaking the tops of the trees. Most are unable to resist the urge to bundle up and step into a storm, to walk against the wind and squint at the sea spray on their faces.

The storms at Long Beach brew in the Bering Sea and Gulf of Alaska, swirling counter-clockwise as they move down the coast. In November, December and February the most savage gales ar-rive, following one after another, eventually attacking the west coast of Vancouver Island from the southeast. At Tofino they've been known to blow 100 kilometres an hour, with gusts to 130. They swell the seas to more than three metres and carry in great masses of moisture, dumping it on forests of hemlock, cedar, sitka spruce and amabalis and grand fir. Half of the 3,226 millimetres of rain that lands on Tofino each year falls between November and February.

With the storms come myriad treasures and with the treas-ures come scores of beachcombers. Though scouring the beaches for items from the deep is among the most fascinating pastimes at Long Beach, it is only one of many. The rugged shores are known by people from around the world who come for different reasons in different seasons. They come to watch the Pacific gray whales on their annual migration between California and Alaska. Others come to photograph the wintering birds, the sea lions and animals of the rain forests. They come to hike the boardwalks and trails, windsurf and kayak in the breakers, to scuba dive in Barkley Sound and the inlets at Tofino and Ucluelet, and to camp beneath the trees and on the beaches. They come to listen to the surf pounding at the headlands and foaming across the sand, to breathe the fragrant sea air, to wander past the fishboats moored at the village docks, and to be mesmerized by the neverending motion of the sea. And they come to reaffirm their belief in pre-serving and sharing this magnificent place forever.

When it was announced that Long Beach would become the

feature attraction in western Canada's first national marine park, many of Vancouver Island's die-hard beach bums openly expressed their discontent. They believed the inevitable invasion of tourists would destroy the solitude, damage the beaches and ruin the wilderness atmosphere that enticed people here in the first place. But the 500,000 annual visitors don't all arrive at once and only a fifth of them come between late autumn and early spring. Anyone who takes a stroll along that endless shoreline can see that nothing natural has really changed: the swollen seas roll in from the open Pacific, the tides come and go, the surf is deafening and the remaining rain forests are as green and luxuriant as they were in the last century. We couldn't have kept Long Beach a secret forever.

Long Beach

TO LONG BEACH BY LAND, SEA OR AIR

The simplest way to get to Long Beach is by road: it's 195 kilometres by road from Nanaimo, 305 kilometres from Victoria. All highways, including Highway 4 between Port Alberni and Long Beach, which was named Pacific Rim Highway in 1985, are paved, but chains or snow tires should be used in winter. Island

Coach Lines runs buses from major Island centres to Port Alberni several times a day. Orient Stage Lines carries passengers between Port Alberni and the Long Beach area. Taxis and rental vehicles are also available.

The Ministry of Transport operates a small airport at Tofino with three concrete runways of 1,525 metres. It's not illuminated for night landing and jet fuel is available. Pacific Rim Airlines flies between Vancouver and Port Alberni, Nanaimo, Ucluelet, Bamfield and Tofino. It also has scheduled float plane flights from Tofino to Ahousat, Hot Springs Cove and several other coastal points. Charter services and short scenic flights out of Tofino are available. The airline's operations are based in Port Alberni with a suboffice near the government wharf in Tofino.

During summer the *Lady Rose*, a 31-metre cargo and passenger ship, operated by Alberni Marine Transportation Incorporated, runs between Port Alberni and Ucluelet. For more on the *Lady Rose* see p.99 .

A growing number of bicyclists are peddling to Long Beach, taking a loop trip using the *Lady Rose* and Highway 4 between Long Beach and Port Alberni. Many start from B.C. Ferry terminals at Nanaimo or Swartz Bay, outside Victoria. There's a picturesque backroads route that follows the eastern side of Vancouver Island as far as Parksville, before cutting across the Island to Port Alberni. The route nearly eliminates the need to travel on Highways 1 and 19 yet it takes only a few minutes longer.

BACKROADS FOR BICYCLES — VICTORIA TO LONG BEACH

There's little point in bicycling, or driving, up Vancouver Island's highways 1 and 19, when the best scenery is found along a backroads route which follows the eastern shoreline. Highway 1 to Nanaimo, and Highway 19 from Nanaimo to Parksville and beyond, are shameful eyesores, their roadsides littered with defunct boat-building businesses, auto wreckers, dry-land log dumps, sawdust storage fields and other unsightly operations. Summer traffic is heavy and crosswinds are a nuisance to bicyclists.

The backroads route from Victoria, however, runs between the highway and the east coast of the Island, through pastoral farmlands, along the shores of Georgia Strait, between Vancouver Island and the mainland. There are good views of the Gulf Islands and several beach accesses.

Cyclists should be wary of log haulers and other large trucks which use some of the backroads. If a truck follows you up a hill,

46

then passes, beware of other vehicles behind the truck: they're not likely to see you until the truck has passed.

Mile zero on this backroads route is the B.C. Ferry terminal at Mill Bay, about 45 kilometres north of Victoria on Highway 1. Some cyclists may choose to ride over the Malahat Mountain, between Victoria and Mill Bay. Those who do should turn right at the north end of the Malahat, following signs to Bamberton Provincial Park. The ferry terminal is a short distance beyond the park entrance. Wise riders will board the ferry at Brentwood Bay, near Butchart Gardens outside Victoria. It's a 24-kilometre journey from the centre of Victoria to the terminal. To reach it take West Saanich Road, which is Highway 17A, and turn left on Verdier Road in the community of Brentwood Bay.

If you're traveling from the B.C. Ferry terminal at Swartz Bay, turn right on Wain Road shortly after leaving the terminal, then turn left on West Saanich Road. Ride 13 kilometres to Verdier Road and turn right. The ferry terminal is at the bottom of the hill.

The cruise across Saanich Inlet takes about 25 minutes. As you leave the ferry at Mill Bay turn right and ride 5.3 kilometres along the shore to a traffic light on Highway 1. Turn right and stay on the highway for 1.4 kilometres, then turn right at Kilmalu Road. After half a kilometre take the first left on Telegraph Road and after 8.8 kilometres turn right onto Cowichan Bay Road and ride 5.9 kilometres around the head of the bay to the Cowichan Indian reserve. Go straight ahead for 5.2 kilometres on Tzouhalem Road through the reserve and turn right on Maple Bay Road. Peddle for 6.2 kilometres and as you come down the hill toward Maple Bay, turn left onto Herd Road.

Stay on Herd for 2.7 kilometres, then turn right onto Osborn Bay Road toward the village of Crofton. The road ends after 5.3 kilometres where you turn left, up the hill toward the town of Chemainus. A total of 3.8 kilometres from the turnoff at Crofton is an intersection: keep to the right and travel 5.8 kilometres to Chemainus.

A total of 9.6 kilometres beyond Chemainus the backroads return to Highway 1 at Ladysmith. Turn right and go 7.4 kilometres to Brenton-Page Road and turn right again. Ride 1.3 kilometres around the head of Ladysmith Harbor and turn left at the first intersection, up a big hill. After 1.6 kilometres turn right on Cedar Road, peddle another 1.6 kilometres and turn right on Yellow Point Road. After 16 kilometres the road rejoins Cedar Road where you turn right. The road ends after 3 kilometres with the Nanaimo River Bridge on the left. Cross the bridge and after 2.7 kilometres turn right onto Highway 1 in Nanaimo. Ride 5.9 kilometres to the lights at Comox Road, cross the bridge on the highway and turn right onto Stewart Road toward the B.C. Ferry

Terminal at Departure Bay. It's 2.4 kilometres to the terminal.

People who arrive on the Island at Nanaimo can pick up the backroads route at Departure Bay. From the bottom of the hill outside the terminal follow the signs up the hill toward Parksville. At the intersection a kilometre up the hill stay to the right onto Departure Bay Road and travel 2.1 kilometres along the edge of the bay before turning right on Hammond Bay Road. Ride 10.1 kilometres and turn right on Applecross Road where you'll see the highway about 100 metres ahead.

After 800 metres turn left on Dover Road, ride 600 metres and turn right on Dickinson Road. Take Lantzville Road on the right after 2.2 kilometres, ride another 3.7 kilometres and turn right on the highway. Follow the shore of Nanoose Harbor for 6.2 kilometres, then turn right onto Northwest Bay Road after crossing a bridge. Stay to the left at an intersection you'll encounter after 3 kilometres and ride 6.1 kilometres to the highway.

The backroads route ends here, about 5 kilometres south of Parksville. From this intersection turn right, then take the turnoff to the left onto Highway 4 to Port Alberni, a distance of 47 kilometres.

The *Lady Rose*, a 31-metre cargo and passenger ship, leaves Port Alberni first thing in the morning. You can walk your bicycle aboard and tie it to a rail on deck. The ship travels through the Broken Group Islands, in Barkley Sound, to Ucluelet and drops passengers traveling to Long Beach. You can spend a few days exploring the Long Beach area and either return on the *Lady Rose* or ride out over the Mackenzie Range. For more detail on the *Lady Rose* see p. 99 .

The 110-kilometre ride through the mountains from Long Beach to Port Alberni should be tackled only by cyclists who've had a lot of recent practice. The road winds though the upper Kennedy River Valley and climbs to more than 300 metres in a number of places. Hills are long with several blind spots. It's advisable to begin the trip at first light to avoid heavy traffic. The journey, in spite of the hardships, is beautiful.

Like hikers, campers and boaters on the west coast, cyclists should be prepared for unwelcome changes in weather. Good wet-weather clothing should be carried and gear should be packed in plastic bags before being loaded onto a bike.

BACK ROADS IN BRIEF

Here's an abbreviated form of the backroads route between Mill Bay and Parksville. You could photocopy it and tape it to a carrying bag or to the dashboard of a car.

Kilometre	Location	Turn
0	Mill Bay	right
5.3	Highway 1	right
6.7	Kilmalu Road	right
7.2	Telegraph Road	left
16.0	Cowichan Bay Road	right
21.9	Tzouhalem Road	straight
27.1	Maple Bay Road	right
33.3	Herd Road	left
36.0	Osborn Bay Road	right
41.3	to Chemainus	left
45.1	intersection	right
50.9	Chemainus	straight
60.5	Highway 1 (Ladysmith)	right
67.9	Brenton-Page Road	right
69.2	intersection	left
70.8	Cedar Road	right
72.4	Yellow Point Road	right
88.4	Cedar Road	right
91.4	Nanaimo River Bridge	left
94.1	Highway 1	right
100.0	Comox Road	right (after bridge)
102.4	Departure Bay Ferry	left
103.4	intersection	right
105.5	Hammond Bay Road	right
115.6	Applecross Road	right
116.4	Dover Road	left
117.0	Dickinson Road	right
119.2	Lantzville Road	right
122.9	Highway 19	right
129.1	Northwest Bay Road	right
132.1	intersection	left
138.2	Highway 19	take Highway 4 to Port Alberni

INFORMATION — HELPFUL ADVICE FOR NEWCOMERS

It's almost impossible for tourists to get lost in the Long Beach area. As you approach the park an information centre, operated during summer by the Tofino and Ucluelet Chambers of Commerce, is located on the Pacific Rim Highway at the Ucluelet-Tofino-Port Alberni junction. The Chambers of Commerce also operate tourist centres in the villages.

For interesting and current information about Pacific Rim and the issues affecting the fortunate few who inhabit this scenic area, publications such as weekly newspapers and locally- produced tourist guides are available. Most of these journals carry a good balance of helpful stories and advertisements. These publications are well worth checking for specific information on whale-watching and nature cruises, fishing and scuba charters, restaurants, art galleries, accommodation, car rentals, local events, shopping facilities and other commercial outlets and activities.

As many as 60,000 people a year may pass the portals of Pacific Rim Park's information centre, located on Highway 4, 2.4 kilometres north of the Ucluelet-Tofino-Port Alberni junction. Open from spring to fall, the centre has displays and a variety of publications. The staff can answer questions about any part of the park, including the Broken Group Islands and West Coast Trail, as well as areas outside Pacific Rim's boundaries. Up-to-date lists of accommodation and charter boat operators should be available. The cedar building is accessible to people in wheelchairs.

People who want information about the Pacific Rim area before traveling to the west coast can write to the addresses shown on p. 177.

ACCOMMODATION AND CAMPING

There are more than two dozen resorts, lodges, motels, hotels, campgrounds and trailer parks in the Long Beach area and nearly all are booked to capacity throughout the tourist season. It would be unwise to arrive at Long Beach without reservations, especially if you're traveling between spring and autumn or on holiday weekends during the year.

With the exception of Parks Canada's campgrounds, all accommodation in the Long Beach area is outside the park, in Tofino and Ucluelet and at points between the park and villages. There are exceptionally beautiful beachfront properties between the north end of Long Beach and Tofino. The accommodation is as varied as the quality, from roadside motels to rustic oceanfront cabins and bed and breakfast stops. In Ucluelet there's even a retired research ship which has been converted to a floating hotel. Some resorts offer both cabins and campsites, a convenient combination for travelers who want to spend a few days in a tent and a night or two in a seaside cottage.

Rowboats and fishing skiffs are available at a few resorts along with ice, fish-freezing facilities, bait and tackle. Fishing, diving and touring charters can be arranged with the help of proprietors. Amenities offered by accommodation owners are extensive: whirlpools, hot tubs, saunas, racquet ball courts, exercise rooms, laundromats, barbecues, fireplaces, kitchenettes, telephones and televisions. Hotels in Tofino and Ucluelet have dining rooms, coffee shops and pubs.

The most reliable source for up-to-date accommodation listings is the B.C. Ministry of Tourism's *Accommodation Guide*. Other accommodation information may be available from local tourist bureaus and chambers of commerce. Most tenters begin camping on Vancouver Island's west coast around Easter weekend. Although the sun may shine for weeks at a time on Long Beach, campers should be prepared for heavy rains at any time of year. Tenters need good flies or plastic tarps. Parks Canada has two permanent campgrounds at Long Beach. They run on a first-come-first-served basis and maximum allowed stay is seven days. They're open year-round and fees are charged between spring and autumn.

Schooner beach camping area

51

The park's main campground is at Green Point, halfway between Schooner Cove and Wickaninnish Beach. There are 93 campsites at Green Point, set in the trees high above the beach where the soothing sounds of the surf lull campers to sleep. Between 11 p.m. and 7 a.m. campers are asked to observe a "quiet time," a few hours of peace for people who'd rather listen to the waves and winds than parties and ghetto blasters. But it's a popular spot: during summer, cars and motor homes line the highway outside the campground entrance, hours before the 11 a.m. checkout time. Among the amenities are washrooms with hot and cold water, picnic tables, fireplaces, firewood and the 230-seat Green Point Theatre. The entrance to Green Point campground is 12.8 kilometres north of the Ucluelet-Tofino-Port Alberni highway junction.

Parks Canada also allows up to 80 tents to be pitched on Long Beach near Schooner Cove, toward the northwest end of the park. Camping here is basic, the only facilities being water and outhouses. The beach at Schooner Cove stretches 2.5 kilometres between Portland Point on the west and Box Island, which can be reached by foot at low tides, on the east. The beach is accessible from an overnight parking lot by an 800-metre trail and boardwalk which takes about 15 minutes to hike. It's the last easily accessible beach at the north end of Pacific Rim Park. People can't drive to this spot and although dozens of campers may set up on the beach, there's a feeling of isolation from the rest of the Long Beach area. Small, dry gullies in rock outcroppings high above the high-tide line provide a few private spots for one or two tents, away from the main beach where campsites may be laid a few steps apart. It's not wilderness camping by any means, but certainly closer to nature than the trailers and motor homes at Green Point: it's a matter of preference. Both are good places to stay.

UCLUELET AND TOFINO —
TWO INTRIGUING TOWNS

Tofino and Ucluelet, at opposite ends of Long Beach, are incorporated fishing, logging, and more recently, tourist villages with all the amenities required by about 3,400 residents from the two communities and surrounding areas. Bakeries, banks, beauty salons, churches, clothing stores, dry cleaners and laundromats, flower shops, gifts and souvenirs, native and local arts and crafts, groceries, hardware, liquor, photo supplies, restaurants, service stations, marinas and public wharves, post offices, a government agent, realtors, police, dental and medical services, pharmacies, taxis, an airport, and tourist information are available. There's even a golf course off Highway 4 on the road to Grice Bay.

Federal government wharves, distinguished by their bright red gangways, are bustling with boatmen during the herring and salmon seasons at Ucluelet and Tofino. Anyone who likes boats and tales of the sea can poke around the floats and chat with fishermen and deck hands. Fresh seafood is often sold year-round off boats moored at government wharves. Some wharves have bulletin boards where information on fishing regulations, scuba, nature and salmon charters, boat rentals and moorage may be obtained. These public wharves are also favored hot spots for youngsters who lie bellies-down and jig for perch or tommy cod that lurk in the shadows of the pilings.

Ucluelet — Gateway to Barkley Sound

Ucluelet, the larger community with a population of about 1,700, sits on the eastern side of Ucluth Peninsula about a third of the way up Ucluelet Inlet from the entrance to Barkley Sound. First-time visitors to Ucluelet are inevitably taken by surprise at the sight of the *Canadian Princess*, an historic west coast steamship which has become a floating hotel. The 70-metre vessel is permanently moored in downtown Ucluelet and used as a base for nature cruises and fishing trips. She was formerly the *William J. Stewart*, a Canadian Hydrographic Service ship used to chart the B.C. coast for 46 years. In 1980 she was converted to her present condition with staterooms for 80 guests, a dining room, lounge and bar. Although fully equipped to run, she stays in Ucluelet as mother ship for several launches which carry passengers into Barkley Sound to search for whales, sea lions, scenery and salmon.

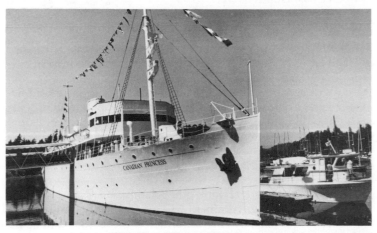

Canadian Princess *at Ucluelet*

Amphitrite Point, on the southern tip of Ucluth Peninsula, is an important centre for ships plying the waters of western Vancouver Island. The Canadian Coast Guard provides marine communications and vessel traffic services from a building next to Amphitrite Point Lighthouse. Often more than a hundred ships are watched on radar as they enter the system's coverage area. They're notified of positions of other ships and potential hazards. Marine advisories and notices to ships are broadcast regularly from the centre.

A whistle buoy marks Carolina Channel at the entrance to Ucluelet Inlet. Waves compress air in the buoy and activate the whistle, producing a foghorn-like sound to aid passing ships. You can hear it from Amphitrite Point.

At the end of 1905 the four-masted barque *Pass of Melfort* met an untimely end on the eastern side of Amphitrite Point. En route from Panama to Port Townsend, Washington, the unfortunate ship was swept ashore and bashed to bits against the rocks. Indians had reported seeing signal flares in the night, but by the time anyone could see the ship her 26 crewmen were dead, their corpses floating amongst the debris of the wreck. Only two battered bodies were recovered from the pounding surf. Scuba divers have since found pieces of the wreck, including an enormous anchor.

Amphitrite Point Lighthouse, established during that same year, has a commanding view over the open Pacific and toward the islands of Barkley Sound. People can stroll around the lighthouse on paved paths: it's particularly invigorating on stormy days. It's also a pleasant place for summer sunsets. To get there drive south through Ucluelet on Ucluth Peninsula Road and turn right on Coast Guard Drive.

Tofino — Gateway to Clayoquot Sound

Although the population of Tofino, 40 kilometres northwest of Ucluelet, is about 1,000, another 700-odd people inhabit surrounding shores and islands. Some are squatters left over from the days of beach-bumming at Florencia Bay; others are landowners or lease holders. They live around Clayoquot Sound in boats or cabins built with materials from the forests and beaches. Tofino is a supply station for many of these people, a place to enjoy some downtown companionship before stocking up and returning to their seclusion. For others it's a gateway to markets, a place for fishermen and oyster farmers to sell or ship their wares — salmon, cod, halibut, prawns, crabs and other shellfish.

One of Tofino's government wharves is known locally as the crab dock and is used by crab fishermen to store traps and tie up their boats. Much of the delicious Dungeness crab they harvest

Tofino

from nearby waters is shipped to markets throughout the Pacific northwest: if you happen to be there when a crab fisherman arrives, you could buy some fresh from the traps, still kicking and complaining, ready for the pot.

Among Tofino's most fascinating features is its West Coast Maritime Museum. Established in 1969 to house a private collection of west coast artifacts, the museum has since accepted numerous donations and loans of nautical paraphernalia and historic items depicting the colorful, and often difficult, lifestyles of earlier generations.

With the advent of Pacific Rim National Park, tourism in these tiny towns has begun to rival fishing and logging as a bread-and-butter industry. When the highway from Port Alberni was paved in 1972 the changes happened quickly. And they're continuing to occur — new resorts and campgrounds, businesses expanding and starting anew. Some residents consider tourists trespassers and resent them; others accept tourism as a legitimate excuse to preserve the natural environment that lures them, an argument against clear-cutting centuries-old timber. Cutting the trees at places like Meares Island, which dominates the village of Tofino, is like killing the last of the dinosaurs: extinction is final.

Tourists may unwittingly be affected by local issues, particularly environmental issues. The people who've chosen a life of semi-isolation in this magnificent wilderness are justifiably wary of changes that alter their surroundings. Visitors should respect the fact that not everyone here is on holiday, and be grateful for the untiring efforts of local residents to keep their home attractive, for both themselves and newcomers.

POLICE AND MEDICAL SERVICES

In case of an emergency in the Long Beach area the simplest thing to do is call a B.C. Telephone Company operator and ask for help. Ambulance services are available and there are medical clinics in Tofino and Ucluelet. Tofino also has a small general hospital. The Royal Canadian Mounted Police have detachments in Ucluelet and Tofino with high-speed boats to police areas not accessible by road, such as Hot Springs Cove or Gibson Marine Park.

WATER, WASHROOMS AND WHEELCHAIRS

Washrooms in Pacific Rim Park are located at all major parking areas and campgrounds. Handicap washrooms are available at the Wickaninnish Centre, the information centre, Green Point parking area, the second parking lot at the Wickaninnish day-use area and the first parking lot at the Long Beach day-use area.

There's a boardwalk for wheelchairs to Wickaninnish Beach at the second parking lot. Long Beach day-use area is accessible to people in wheelchairs from the second parking lot. A viewing platform for wheelchairs has been built at Radar Hill. Wheelchairs can be used on all of the 800-metre Shorepine Bog Trail.

Outdoor water taps are located at Green Point, at Wickaninnish Beach in the sheltered cooking area and behind the washrooms in the second parking lot, and in the second parking lot at Combers Beach.

DOGS — RESPECT OTHERS

One of the pleasures of owning a dog is watching it run free on an open beach, dig in the sand and wade the shallow waters of an isolated bay. Not everyone, however, is a dog lover and the rights of those people should be respected. No one would suggest that a dog be kept leashed everywhere around Long Beach, but in busy beach areas, population centres, in campgrounds and on hiking trails it is not unreasonable to expect dog owners to control their pets. Dogs are not allowed to run loose in Pacific Rim Park but they can bound up and down the beaches outside the park. Most resort and campground owners, however, discourage people from bringing dogs to their establishments. If you turn your dog loose on a beach don't let it foul heavily-used areas or disturb other beachcombers and frighten children.

Dogs at Pacific Rim are also known to run deer and chase shorebirds, many which are resting and feeding while migrating to wintering or nesting grounds.

THE CAMPFIRE — A PLACE FOR FRIENDS TO GATHER

A campfire is the centre of every campsite, a gathering place to barbecue steaks or salmon fillets, roast weiners or marshmallows, warm a pot of coffee and discuss the issues of the day. On clear, moonlit summer nights at Long Beach there's little more satisfying than huddling around a beach fire under a profusion of stars, listening to the surf and the crackle of burning driftwood.

Fires in Pacific Rim Park are allowed on the beach below the winter high-tide mark, easily recognized by the lines of flotsam and driftwood at the top of the beach. They can also be lit in established fire pits in campgrounds. Cut firewood is provided free for registered campers at Green Point campground from Easter to Thanksgiving weekend. Common sense and courtesy are expected of people who light fires: use them for cooking and cuddling but don't burn up half the wood on the beach and don't set bonfires in the drift logs. Never leave a fire unattended: a breeze could scatter sparks and coals. The fire must be extinguished so coals are cold enough to pick up with your bare hand.

Fires are banned in some areas, which are usually signposted. The B.C. Forest Service also prohibits fires during periods of extreme drought and advertises the prohibitions on radio, television and in newspapers. They're strictly enforced and fines or jail terms may be ordered for offenders. People who cause a fire through carelessness or violation of laws can be ordered to pay costs of damage and fighting the fire, a figure which could be hundreds of thousands of dollars.

The B.C. Forest Service has a toll-free telephone number to call and report forest fires. Anyone who spots what appears to be a forest fire is asked to call the operator and ask for Zenith 5555.

Enjoy your campfire, but be careful.

SURF SAFETY — BE OCEANWISE

For generations Long Beach has been known as the surfing capital of Canada. Those giant breakers rolling onto the sandy shores rival the surfing conditions of southern California, though

57

the nippy seas are admittedly not as inviting. From late spring to early fall water temperatures rarely exceed 14 degrees celsius and often drop below 9 degrees. But in spite of the cold, a few courageous swimmers, clad only in bathing suits, plunge into the waves and ride the crests back to shore.

Most surfers, kayakers and sailboarders, however, wear full wet suits or wet suit tops. A swimmer without a wet suit might last half an hour or 45 minutes before becoming hypothermic: a wet suit may allow a swimmer to splash around the surf for half the day.

Conventional surfing has always been popular at Long Beach and in recent years windsurfing and surf kayaking have taken off. Competitions in all three sports are held at Long Beach and as the popularity of these sports grows, so too will Long Beach as an exciting place to practise them. Check at the park information centre or local tourist bureaus to see if kayaks, surfboards and sailboards are available for rent.

Anyone who dabbles in the surf should be familiar with the dangers of rip currents, swiftly moving water which can sweep you out to sea. Currents that flow parallel to beaches may turn directly toward the open ocean when they hit rock formations. At Long Beach the worst ones occur at Wickaninnish, Green Point and near the large offshore rock in front of the Long Beach parking lot. They're also dangerous at either end of Florencia Bay.

People on air mattresses or inner tubes have a habit of getting sucked away by these currents. If you get caught in one, swim parallel to the beach until you are out of its force then head directly for shore. Currents can carry you along the shore so keep an eye on your position along the beach when swimming with the current.

Breakers are powerful, hazardous forces that can push you under and roll you around as they slide up the beaches. If you get dumped from a surfboard or kayak, stay seaward of it until you're sure it's not going to come crashing down on your head. Then get back on and keep trying. Life jackets, for both kids and adults, not only make a swim at Long Beach safer but improve buoyancy for body surfing.

During summer, surf guards are posted at the northern end of Long Beach, near the parking lot. They rescue struggling surfers and swimmers by paddling out on surfboards. Surf guards maintain radio contact with park wardens and inflatable rescue boats can be launched if necessary. They're not babysitters, however, and people who challenge the Long Beach breakers are expected to take sensible precautions. Never leave children unattended near breaking waves or by rocky headlands which have rip currents running along their edges, and never swim alone.

Wickaninnish Centre

THE WICKANINNISH CENTRE

The Wickaninnish Centre, once a celebrated seafront inn, is an ocean interpretation centre which opened in the summer of 1984. It's located on Wickaninnish Beach, eight kilometres from the park entrance, and is designed to accommodate visitors in wheelchairs. Two observation decks with telescopes overlook Wickaninnish Beach. The centre is open during the day from late spring to early fall.

The most striking feature is an immense mural — 24 metres by 6 metres — depicting 75 life-sized creatures of the deep, including a 12-metre humpback whale and a 3-metre blue shark. A smaller mural portrays 15 seabird species.

The centre's purpose is to provide an understanding of the north Pacific Ocean, its influence on nature and man. You can take an imaginary journey to infrequently-traveled depths aboard the *Explorer 10*, a replica of a deep-sea submersible with portholes looking toward a three-dimensional model of the ocean floor. The *Explorer 10* probes depths of less than a kilometre but the smaller *Cascadia* is capable of deeper dives. A television monitor aboard the *Explorer 10* relays scenes of a descent being made by the *Cascadia*, complete with conversation between scientists inside the two submersibles. The monitor shows the *Cascadia's* descent from a depth of 580 metres as it follows the profile of the Delwood Seamount, an underwater mountain 400 kilometres northwest of the Wickaninnish Centre.

A 25-minute film, *Great Ocean*, shown every hour in the centre's 60-seat theatre, gives an insight into some of the mysteries of the Pacific, the largest and deepest body of water on earth. The history of the North Pacific coast is illustrated by a collection of artifacts used by Nuu-chah-nulth Indians, the traditional inhabitants of the area. The collection includes an 11-metre whaling canoe.

The Wickaninnish Centre was planned since the mid-1970s but construction didn't begin until 1979. The building was completed in 1981, the displays in 1983. Of the original Wickaninnish Inn, only the lounge, with its distinctive saddle-shaped roof, has been retained and converted to a restaurant.

NATURALIST PROGRAMS — DISCOVERING A HERITAGE

The park naturalists at Long Beach are a dedicated bunch who work hard to enhance the holidays of visitors to Pacific Rim Park. Their enthusiasm is contagious as they meet groups in the rain forests, take them on hunts in the intertidal zones or help them explore rocky tide pools. Their services are offered free to anyone interested in the natural and human history of Long Beach. To see what's happening check at the park information centre and on bulletin boards around Long Beach, particularly at Green Point campground.

During a typical week the events on an agenda for naturalist programs may look like this: a campfire talk on the native Indians who once inhabited the shores of Long Beach and how they lived before the arrival of the white man; a tide pool talk on the fascinating strategies for survival of sea stars, mussels, anemones and other intertidal creatures; a journey to Grice Bay mudflats to stretch a beach seine across the shallows and catch animals that live in the eel grass; a family gathering at the Rain Forest Trail for all kinds of activities, including bark-rubbing and testing the pH of the soil; a walk to a sheltered cove where scuba divers may come to the surface with urchins, sea cucumbers, crabs and other creatures of the deep so everyone can have a closer look. The naturalists, to the delight of parents, even organize special children's events, with personified crab races on the beach.

There are also nightly programs in the 230-seat Green Point Theatre, located in the campground. Movies, lectures, concerts and audio-visual programs are offered in the early evening so little campers can crawl into their sleeping bags at a reasonable hour. You may learn of the shipwrecks that gave this coast the ominous title, Graveyard of the Pacific; a slide show about the night sky at Long Beach may be followed by a stroll on the beach with an astronomer; films and talks on birds and wildlife, early pioneers, Indians, sea monsters and the drama of intertidal survival are among the topics presented in the Green Point Theatre.

For people who prefer to explore the natural features of Pacific Rim on their own, Parks Canada has produced a number of publications to help. Gray whales, sea lions and other marine mammals, geology, trees and shrubs, intertidal life, ocean currents and tides are covered in various brochures. Special publications on certain trails are often available at trail heads and bird watchers can pick up a checklist of about 250 species known to occur in and around Pacific Rim Park. The *Pacific Rim Fun Book*, with puzzles and seashore riddles, pictures to color, games and quizzes, has been published for children. Information on bear hazards, red tide and sport fishing is also available.

The programs at Long Beach are extremely well organized by professional naturalists, yet they're presented in an informal way. Many vacationing families plan their days around the naturalist activities, taking advantage of these free and informative services to make the most of their holidays at the beach. But like all government services, Pacific Rim's naturalist programs are at the mercy of budgetary decisions made by politicians on the other side of Canada. It would be a shame to see these valuable programs cut, or possibly eliminated, in the interest of saving a few dollars. Some families rarely get a chance to visit the sea: the naturalist programs not only add color and intrigue to their vacations, they promote a conservation ethic, an appreciation of the need to preserve these wonderful gifts of nature.

WHALE WATCHING — A PLEASANT ADDICTION

When the Pacific gray whales pass the coast of southern Vancouver Island on their 10,000-kilometre northward migration, hundreds of curious naturalists converge on the shores of Long Beach. Dressed in winter woollies and rain gear they travel to the most accessible points and gather on rocky promontories and beaches. They set up spotting scopes or watch through binoculars from the headlands near Schooner Cove, from Quisitis and Wya points. Others ensconce themselves on Combers Beach in the hopes of seeing gray whales feeding in the shallows near Sea Lion Rocks. Parks Canada has mounted telescopes at Radar Hill, the Wickaninnish Centre and on the rocks at Green Point to view the whales and other marine life.

Pacific gray whales, unlike most of the 21 other whale species that occupy western Canadian oceans, migrate within viewing distance of shore. From late February until May an estimated

61

17,000 grays parade past Pacific Rim Park: on calm, clear days whale watchers may see more than a dozen an hour pass within a kilometre of shore.

Whale watching at Long Beach has become so popular that at least a dozen boat charter outfits offer tours of the best viewing areas. Information on the whales of Pacific Rim, as well as a current list of charter boat operators offering whale watching tours may also be available in the park.

During the peak of the grays' migration, whale watching requires a great deal of patience as well as tolerance to cold sea breezes and frequent downpours. Warm winter clothing and good quality wet-weather wear are imperative for comfortable days near the pounding surf and sea spray of the west coast. Telescopes and camera equipment should be protected from water by wrapping them in plastic bags or using an umbrella. Once you get settled you may want to spend several hours in one place so pack a lunch and something warm to drink.

Anyone who's seen wild whales can quickly develop a mild obsession with them. It must be their utter immensity that gives these great leviathans such spellbinding powers. They have an uncanny ability to excite the imagination of anybody who sees one simply surface for a breath of air. A whale sighting near a crowded beach is an event that draws total strangers to one another's campfires to talk enthusiastically about the prospect of seeing one again. Experienced west coast beachcombers often catch themselves unconsciously searching beyond the surf for spurts of willowy mist: they've seen these behemoths before. They're addicted.

Easter, the start of the coastal camping season, is prime time for whale watching at Long Beach. It's then that the Pacific gray whale's migration — one of the longest of any mammal on earth — reaches its peak. Their arrival is predictable, like salmon homing in on their spawning grounds. The first whales show in late February but gale-force storms and pitiless rains often dissuade would-be whale watchers from setting up viewing stations on wave-whipped headlands. A month or six weeks later, when seas are calmer and weather's warmer, the whales arrive in droves and pass one or two kilometres offshore. Occasionally they're seen 100 metres or so from land but most sightings are somewhere just beyond the breaking surf. The best time is early morning when whale spouts can be seen clearly above the surface. By late morning or afternoon, winds flatten the spouts and mix them with whitecaps, making them difficult to spot.

On still days the blast from a gray whale's blowholes can be heard a kilometre away as it shoots nearly 5 metres in the air. Though it has two blowholes the spout appears as a single,

Pacific gray whale flashes its flukes

vertical column, occasionally divided at the top. If it's diving in deep water, say more than 40 metres, it may blow five or six times, vanish for 7, 8, perhaps 10 minutes then resurface half a kilometre away. When it dives it rolls forward, exposing a series of bumps, or "knuckles," on the lower back where most other whale species have dorsal fins. The tail flukes are usually visible only before a deep dive. For shallow dives a gray whale may take three   or four breaths at intervals of 10 or 20 seconds before diving for 3 or 4 minutes. It'll reappear about 300 metres away if it's migrating but will stay in the area if feeding. When swimming in shallow waters gray whales appear pale, almost white on sunny days.

If you can get close enough to look a gray whale in the eye, as some courageous boaters do, you'll see blotches of barnacles on the skin, particularly around the head. One barnacle species uses only the gray whale as its habitat. It's difficult to see its fuzzy snout and irregular rows of hairy bristles growing on the top of the head and along the side of the lower jaw. You'll likely be surprised if the whale decides to do some spy-hopping while you're there. A gray whale's eyes are more than two metres from its nose so if it wants to see you it must hoist its bulky body straight up by beating its tail underwater, or in shallow water, by resting its flukes on the bottom. It may hold this position half a minute and turn a full circle before breaching two or three times and diving. They frequently spy-hop at the sound of approaching boats.

Pacific grays feed infrequently on their long migrations between southern California or Mexico and the Gulf of Alaska. Many migrants, however, stop to feed for a few days off Vancouver Island as they travel north. About 40 grays that remain off southwest Vancouver Island for the summer seem perpetually surrounded by churned-up sand. They're feeding in the shallows, ploughing along the bottom, stirring up sediment and sucking up crustaceans, molluscs and bristle worms. Occasionally they'll surface with jaws full of mud. They also feed at times on tiny shrimp-like organisms in the water column, particularly along the West Coast Trail and in Barkley Sound.

It's remarkable that such titanic animals subsist on such minute organisms. Pacific grays are baleen whales, adapted to filter out tiny prey through a series of plates which grow down from the roof of the mouth. Similar in chemical composition to the human fingernail, the outer edges of the baleen are smooth while the inner edges are lined with bristles or fibres. The whale sucks in huge quantities of sand, water and food, then pushes it out with the force of a tongue weighing 1,400 kilograms. The bristles on the inner edges of the baleen catch tiny organisms as the water and sand shoots out. Scientists have discovered consistently greater wear of baleen plates and an almost total lack of barnacles on the right side of gray whales, suggesting they swim on that side while feeding. Baleen was used during the 19th century to make stiff corsets and hoops to hold up women's skirts.

The whales that travel the full migration route leave their northern feeding grounds in late September and early October. Pregnant females are followed by other adults and yearlings and they cross the Gulf of Alaska at a speed of about 185 kilometres a day. They become visible from land in early November and late December but rough seas and overcast skies make them difficult to see. Some believe they travel farther offshore on their southerly migration.

By the middle of December they appear off San Francisco and many move into the lagoons of Scammon and San Ignacio on the western side of the Baja Peninsula. It's here in January that the cows, after carrying calves for 12 months, give birth. At the same time bulls perform elaborate courtship rituals to win the affections of available females. They lie bellies together and copulate numerous times for as long as an hour, ending each contact with a massive orgasmic shudder.

Meanwhile, calves weighing from 700 to 1,400 kilograms are born in the same lagoons. Cows defend their young so aggressively that whalers, who once slaughtered them on the breeding grounds, called them devil fish. Feeding on their mothers' milk they gain 25 kilograms a day in preparation for the start of their northward migration in February. By the time a calf is weaned at seven or eight months its length will have doubled to about 9 metres and its body weight will have increased eight times. After they reach sexual maturity at eight years old some cows will give birth to a single calf every year. Others produce offspring every second or third year. By breeding age a female gray whale may measure nearly 13 metres and weigh 31,000 kilograms. A male could be more than 12 metres long and weigh 26,000 kilograms. Many Pacific grays live to be 60 or 80 years old.

Pacific gray whales stand as an example of what can be achieved through drastic conservation measures. In 18 years of west coast whaling the gray whale was hunted to near extinction. Atlantic populations were wiped out decades ago, leaving the Pacific grays as the last remaining race of gray whales on earth. In the 1940s they became protected by international agreement and remain protected today in their migration and summer feeding waters by American and Canadian law. Scammon's Lagoon, one of the principal calving grounds in Mexico, was declared a national whale reserve in 1972. Their comeback has been miraculous, from a few hundred to an estimated 17,000 today.

Some experts believe the burgeoning whale-watching industry poses a threat to whales. The Canadian government has produced a booklet entitled *Whale Watching*, which contains guidelines for observing wild whales. It warns boaters not to chase or disturb resting whales or split up pods. A hundred metres is close enough, according to the guidelines.

For many naturalists whale watching is an annual habit, an addiction that can be satisfied only by packing up and heading for the west coast in spring. We're fortunate we had the sagacity to save these intriguing sea giants before they were lost forever.

LONG BEACH — THE ULTIMATE RUN

Long Beach is a jogger's dream. You can pick a point in the distance and run for miles on hard-packed sand along the edge of the sea. Shoes normally worn on pavement or jogging trails are fine for hard sand: many Long Beach joggers prefer to run barefoot, splashing along in an inch or two of water to stay cool.

The breezes off the sea can be chilly, particularly in early morning or after sunset, so pack a sweat suit and be prepared for rain. For prepared joggers, Long Beach is a pleasant place to run at any time of year.

LONG BEACH HIKING —
BEACHES, BOGS AND BOARDWALKS

The beaches of Pacific Rim have a magnetic appeal that draws people from their cabins, tents and campers toward the sea. Some seek the solitude of walking alone on miles of open, sandy shore; others hike the beaches in the hope of meeting new friends who've come, like themselves, to escape the burdens of city life. Children spend hour upon hour building castles in the sand and jumping the waves as they lap at the shore. These beaches are a captivating combination of unparalleled ocean scenery, salty air and the soothing, constant rhythm of surf against sand.

While many beach hikers look to this coast for emotional satisfaction, others search for something tangible — glass floats, the most prized quarry of west coast beachcombers. They come in all shapes and sizes, from baseball-sized spheres to sausage-shaped tubes as large as a beer bottle. As the number of beachcombers indulging in this pleasant pastime grows, so too does the challenge of finding one.

The glass floats tossed ashore at Long Beach are among thousands lost on the fishing grounds of the North Pacific each year. Most come from Japan where they're carried north along the Asian coast by the Kuroshio Current and across the Pacific by the West Wind Drift. If they don't land on Vancouver Island the first time around, they're carried down the coast of North America by the California Current and back to the North Pacific by the North Equatorial Current. One complete circuit is approximately 24,000 kilometres and some floats make several journeys before falling into the hands of a Vancouver Island beachcomber.

High technology construction at Long Beach

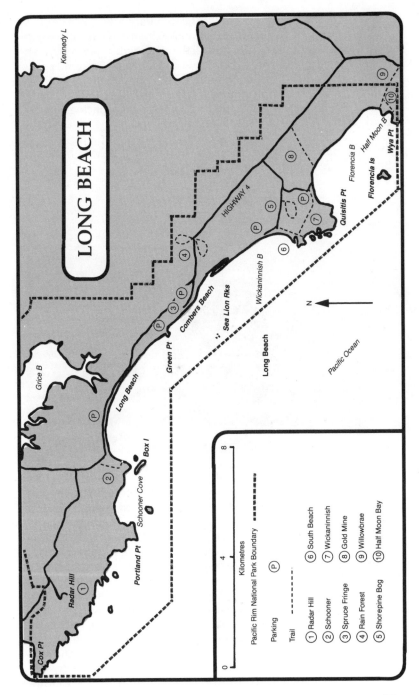

LONG BEACH

Kennedy L

Grice B

LONG BEACH

HIGHWAY 4

Pacific Rim National Park Boundary

Parking ⓟ

Trail

Kilometres

0   4   8

① Radar Hill
② Schooner
③ Spruce Fringe
④ Rain Forest
⑤ Shorepine Bog

⑥ South Beach
⑦ Wickaninnish
⑧ Gold Mine
⑨ Willowbrae
⑩ Half Moon Bay

Cox Pt
Radar Hill ①
Portland Pt
Schooner Cove
Box I
②
Long Beach
Green Pt ⓟ ③ ⓟ ④
Combers Beach
Sea Lion Rks
Long Beach
Wickaninnish B
⑥
⑤ ⓟ
ⓟ ⑦ ⓟ
⑧
Quisitis Pt
Florencia B
Florencia Is
Half Moon B
Wya Pt
⑨
⑩

Pacific Ocean

N

Within the boundaries of Pacific Rim Park hikers can comb a 19-kilometre sandy shore from Schooner Cove in the northwest to Half Moon Bay in the south, a stroll that energetic types can finish in one long day. A route to Schooner Cove begins from the parking lot at the head of the Schooner Trail, an 800-metre path to Schooner beach camping area on the northwest end of Long Beach. Schooner Cove is actually around a point facing Box Island, about 700 metres southwest of the end of the trail. About two kilometres east of the Schooner beach camping area is another parking lot for people visiting Long Beach, between Schooner Cove and Green Point campground.

Drift logs for beachcombers

It was here, directly in front of the Long Beach parking lot, that archeologists, in 1978, attempted to unearth the remains of a so-called mystery ship, the subject of many reported sightings by local residents. For years people claimed to have seen the outline of the ship in the sand after violent storms. There were also stories of ghostly figures stalking the beach near the shipwreck site.

During the 1920s and '30s a university group from the United States frequently visited Long Beach and took wood samples from what appeared to be the planks of a wreck in the sand. The samples were analyzed as oak: Spanish galleons were the only early ships to be made with oak planking and historians surmised that Spanish explorers may have landed at Long Beach before the arrival in 1778 of Captain James Cook, the famous British hydrographer credited with being the first European to set foot on

British Columbia land. One sample of oak taken from the ghost ship was carved into a cribbage board and housed in a Port Alberni museum. Other stories, however, suggest the wood was teak, the material used in construction of Chinese and Japanese junks.

On the basis of old reports, the location of the ship was pinpointed and a physicist searched the area with a magnetometer, hoping to detect metal fittings on the wreck. Positive readings were obtained and a backhoe rolled onto the beach and dug nearly four metres into the sand, only to find an enormous rock outcropping of similar dimensions to the ship.

The ship reported by so many could possibly be the remains of the *Mustang*, a three-masted barque which ran aground on Long Beach in 1866. The brig *William G. Irwin* was also beached in the area in 1887, after being abandoned at sea.

Slightly more than 3 kilometres from the Long Beach parking lot is Green Point, where a telescope is mounted to watch sea lions resting on nearby offshore rocks. A better viewpoint is about 1.5 kilometres beyond Green Point on Combers Beach, directly in front of another parking lot. It's approximately 3.5 kilometres from the Combers Beach parking lot to the Wickaninnish Centre, where a trail and boardwalk cross Quisitis Point, which separates Wickaninnish Beach from Florencia Bay. The 2.5-kilometre Wickaninnish Trail forks to the east, toward Florencia Bay, off the South Beach Trail.

From the parking lot at Florencia Bay it's a four-kilometre hike to the south end of the beach. Here the Willowbrae Trail runs a short distance into the woods before connecting to the Half Moon Bay Trail, which crosses another headland to the most southerly beach in the Long Beach section of the park.

A walk of about two kilometres back up the Half Moon Bay and Willowbrae trails takes you out to Highway 4, two kilometres south of the Ucluelet-Tofino-Port Alberni junction.

Not all of the long sandy beaches of Pacific Rim are located within the park. Beyond Cox Point, at the northwest end of the park are three beautiful beaches with more than five kilometres of shoreline — Cox Bay, Chesterman Beach and MacKenzie Beach.

Besides being extremely attractive, the beaches of Pacific Rim are easy places to walk and it's likely that the majority of people in the area at any time can be found on the beaches. But there are several other natural places to explore along paths and boardwalks both in and outside the park. Most are well-maintained and pose little difficulty for even the most sedentary hikers. And although most of the trails are near popular beaches, hikers often encounter few, if any, other people on the trails.

The hikes within the park boundaries suggested here are

Below Green Point campground

listed as you would find them if you were driving from Tofino to Ucluelet. Equipment normally used by the serious hiker is unnecessary on these trails but rubber or high-topped leather boots may be comfortable if the weather's been wet. Good rain gear, or at least an umbrella, should be carried in case of unwelcome changes in the weather. On hot days bug repellent and water may be handy, and binoculars or spotting scopes are particularly useful at viewpoints and beaches. If you've got space in a pack, do the hikers who follow you a small kindness and pick up any litter you find along the way.

The trails in Pacific Rim Park have been built not only to help hikers discover the natural beauty of the area, but to discourage visitors from wandering off the beaten track. With a growing number of people exploring these areas it's imperative that they be left untouched for future generations. It's a simple courtesy to leave plants, flowers and sea shells for others to see: resist the collector's urge.

Radar Hill

The 96-metre summit of Radar Hill is near the northwest end of the park, 1.4 kilometres up a paved road from Highway 4. It's steep and winding: a small area to unhitch and park trailers has been set aside at the start of the road.

Hikers can either walk up the road from Highway 4 or drive to the top and stroll around paved paths for panoramic views of the islands, forests, inlets and ocean. A telescope is mounted on the peak and a viewing platform has been built for wheelchairs.

On a clear day the views from Radar Hill, an old military installation, are undoubtedly the most spectacular in the Long Beach part of the park. Meares Island, Browning Passage, and the intricate waterways of Tofino Inlet are to the north; Vargas, Flores and Wickaninnish islands to the northwest; and the breakers crashing onto Long Beach and Wickaninnish Bay to the southeast.

Orientation panels have been mounted around the summit. They're paintings depicting the seascape and countryside you see as you stand in front of each picture. Prominent landmarks are numbered on the paintings and keyed to a list of names. The paintings are a novel idea which add interest and education to a visit to Radar Hill.

There's no shelter up here and on gusty days it's often difficult to walk against the wind. For those who step into the storm, Radar Hill is an exhilarating place. Take your binoculars.

Schooner Trail

This 800-metre path leads to Schooner walk-in campground,

Pacific Rim Park's beach camping area with room for about 80 tents. It begins at a large parking lot off Highway 4, at the Tofino end of the park, where overnight parking is allowed. The beach camping area, located on Long Beach near Schooner Cove, is an easy 15-minute walk with stairways and boardwalks and a bridge across a small salmon stream.

Schooner Cove, bounded by Portland Point and Box Island, is the most northwesterly, easily accessible beach in the park. It can be reached by walking from the end of the Schooner Trail at Long Beach, around an unnamed point facing Box Island. A day parking lot is located at Long Beach just over two kilometres east of the point.

In the winter of 1880 the 12-man crew of the barque *General Cobb* was marooned on one of the islets off Schooner Cove after their ship was holed on a reef. They sat on a storm-torn rock for two days before Clayoquot Indians appeared in a large canoe and rescued them. The Indians later were given medals for their courageous assistance.

Spruce Fringe Trail

Parts near the beginning of this 1.5-kilometre boardwalk loop can be used by people in wheelchairs. It begins at the westernmost parking lot for Combers Beach, between Green Point campground and the Wickaninnish Centre.

The sitka spruce is a tenacious conifer able to grow in salty, magnesium-rich soils where most other seedlings die. Winter storms hurl salt and sand high above the driftwood logs and high winds push the spruce branches away from the sea. The ones close to the sea are twisted and eerie, their denuded limbs sometimes covered in moss all the way to the crowns. Ivy and licorice fern entangle the trunks of some. On the lower parts of the trail crabapple and willow thrive, but as the trail moves inland the enormous spruce trees dominate the forest.

This is part of British Columbia's sitka spruce fringe, a wide stretch of spruce which runs up the outer coast of Vancouver Island and the Queen Charlottes, as well as exposed sections of the mainland coast. At this part of Long Beach the sitka spruce fringe is about 200 metres wide.

The forest is exceptionally beautiful as several staircases climb farther up from the shore, deeper into the woods. The trail passes a swampy area with a luxuriance of ferns and skunk cabbage.

Rain Forest Trail

The Rain Forest Trail is actually two loops, each 1.2

kilometres long, on opposite sides of Highway 4, about 6.4 kilometres northwest of the park information centre, or about 3.5 kilometres southeast of Green Point campground.

Rain Forest Trail

This is a virgin forest, a magnificent natural treasure that's vanishing from coastal British Columbia in spite of environmentalists' untiring efforts to preserve what's left. These centuries-old amabalis fir, western redcedar and hemlock humble the lowly hiker who strolls beneath their boughs. The forest floor is strewn with ancient deadfalls, nurse logs where seedlings, fungi and ferns take root and continue the endless cycle. Each time one crashes to the ground, other, smaller trees around it find new light for new growth. Less than 10 percent of the light that shines on this forest canopy reaches the ground, yet even in the absence of direct sunlight no patch of forest floor is barren. Blueberry, huckleberry and salal thickets, deer fern, salmonberry and skunk cabbage grow along the trails. Wildflowers and mosses compete for space, and lichens provide a home for a host of insects. And the insects feed the chickadees and kinglets.

The ages of these enormous evergreens are incredible: cedars more than 800 years old, hemlocks older than 300. Unlike most forests on Vancouver Island, this rain forest has been unscathed by natural fires. It's a foggy, soggy climate at Long Beach and natural fires rarely get a chance to start.

Parks Canada has produced a self-guiding pamphlet on the Rain Forest Trail which is usually available at the trail head.

Shorepine Bog Trail

The Shorepine Bog Trail, on the Wickaninnish Beach Road 300 metres south of the Florencia Bay turnoff, is an 800-metre boardwalk which can be used by people in wheelchairs. It traverses one of the wettest parts of the park where stumpy, tangled trees grow from soggy, moss-covered ground. Though hemlock, yellow cedar and redcedar grow in the bog's acidic soil, shorepine, with its ghostly gray limbs and green clumpy cap, is the dominant species.

These trees are a stark contrast to the towering rain forests which grow in areas of better drainage around Long Beach. The poorly-drained bogs make up about five percent of the Long Beach forest environment. Sphagnum moss builds up on the floor of the bog and absorbs water. It releases organic acids, further hampering the growth of the forest. Hummocks, or islands in the bog, are formed by layers of sphagnum moss piling up around the base of a tree or stump. These areas are drier than the rest of the bog, providing a more hospitable environment for plants such as salal or bunchberry.

Growth of trees in the bog is retarded so severely that some short five-metre pines may be two or three centuries old. Among the plants found in the bog are crowberry, bog cranberry, Labrador tea, bog laurel and the carnivorous sundew, a sticky- leafed

Shorepine Bog Trail

plant that eats insects.

Pacific Rim Park has published a self-guiding pamphlet on the Shorepine Bog Trail. Numbered stops along the trail are keyed to drawings and descriptions in the pamphlet. It is normally available at the start of the trail.

South Beach Trail

A 700-metre trail and boardwalk to South Beach begins at the Wickaninnish Centre. Though only a short distance from the often-crowded shores of Wickaninnish Beach, South Beach is among those Long Beach hideaways where you may find yourself entirely alone in the height of the tourist season.

A few steps from the start of the trail is Lismer Beach, a pebble cove named for Arthur Lismer, one of the famous Group of Seven painters who spent many summers here. Lismer Beach is a good place to explore tide pools at low tides but shells and driftwood should be left intact. Beyond Lismer Beach a boardwalk climbs to the top of a headland with views along Long Beach toward Schooner Cove.

South Beach

The Wickaninnish Trail to Florencia Bay turns to the east from this headland while the South Beach Trail continues straight ahead. A huge rock sits on the beach at the end of the trail, facing a narrow cove where winter waves surge onto the beach. A walk along the beach to the south takes you to a couple of better-protected coves. Fishermen often surf-cast from the shores near the end of the trail.

Wickaninnish Trail

This 2.5-kilometre trail and boardwalk crosses Quisitis Point, which separates Wickaninnish Beach from Florencia Bay. On the Florencia Bay side the trail begins near the parking lot. On the opposite side it starts at a fork off the South Beach Trail, which begins at the Wickaninnish Centre.

This route was part of an overland link between Ucluelet and Tofino which was used until 1942 when the road between the villages was completed. Some of the old cedar slabs laid across the trail are still visible.

The only petroglyphs in the Long Beach area are on a rock face near the end of Quisitis Point. Five animal figures are faintly inscribed in a wall facing Wickaninnish Bay, directly behind a small islet. You can follow the cliffs around the end of the point to find them.

A number of geographic features around Long Beach bear the name of Wickaninnish, a powerful and influential leader of the Clayoquot Indians near the turn of the 18th century. In the late 1700s Wickaninnish made a deal with American seaman John Kendrick in which the chief swapped six muskets, a boat sail, some gunpowder and an American flag for 47 square kilometres of land near Flores Island, northwest of Tofino. The trade included all the islands, mines, minerals, creeks, rivers, bays, harbors, sounds and produce of the sea within the territory.

The great chief earlier had exchanged with Commander John Meares of the Royal Navy two copper tea kettles for about 50 sea otter skins. The value of the pelts to wealthy Chinese mandarins was estimated at more than $100,000.

Gold Mine Trail

This trail is one of the easiest in the park with a gradual 2-kilometre descent to the northwest end of Florencia Bay. A parking lot marks the start of the trail 1.6 kilometres west of the park information centre off Highway 4.

Lost Shoe Creek, which hugs the trail as it approaches the beach, was the site of small placer mining operations in the early 1900s. Gold was discovered in the sand on the beach and claims

At Florencia Bay

were staked in 1899. Many of Ucluelet's original pioneers were lured by tales of gold at Wreck Bay, as it was known then, and a small syndicate was formed. Some reports say more than $20,000 worth of gold was taken from the beach in the early 1900s.

The forest along the trail is a refreshing mixture of red alder and Douglas-fir planted after the area was logged in the 1960s. It hangs over the trail, creating a sylvan tunnel, a pleasant place to walk when the leaves are changing colors in fall. A log bridge crosses Lost Shoe Creek at its mouth and a rusted old mining dredge sits on the bank of the creek.

A weathering, modernistic totem pole stands boldly above the beach near the end of the Gold Mine Trail. Created by four talented beach sculptors, it was raised on July 15, 1971 to honor the child of one artist, a boy who was born on the beach at Florencia Bay. About 150 or 200 squatters lived on the beach at the time. Parks Canada took it down when the squatters were being evicted from the park, but a hex had been put on the totem, a warning to anyone who dared to remove it. It was resurrected shortly after its removal.

Willowbrae Trail

The 2.1-kilometre Willowbrae Trail to Florencia Bay, also known as Wreck Bay, begins outside the park, off Highway 4 to Ucluelet. Two kilometres south of the Ucluelet-Tofino-Port Alberni highway junction is Willowbrae Road. As you head toward Ucluelet turn right up a short gravel road to a parking spot.

Like the Wickaninnish Trail, the Willowbrae Trail was once part of the overland link between Ucluelet and Tofino. Originally wide enough for horse-drawn wagons, it was surfaced with cedar slabs, cut by hand from the surrounding forest.

The beginning of the trail is still wide, skirted by rows of luxuriant sword fern. The forest at the start is open with sparse underbrush, but as the sound of the sea begins to penetrate the air the forest closes in; salal and patches of huckleberry line the trail as it narrows. A boardwalk with a handrail helps hikers down a steep hill to the beach, an amenity most people appreciate when puffing back up the trail. The Half Moon Bay Trail veers to the southwest as the first views of the ocean appear. A creek runs alongside the boardwalk and splashes onto the sand, carving deep grooves to be washed away by the incoming tide.

The path ends on the south end of Florencia Bay, named for a Peruvian brigantine wrecked in the winter of 1861 in a cove on Florencia Islet, which lies two kilometres west of the trail's end. The wrecking ended a terrifying 51-day ordeal for her crew. The ship, laden with lumber and bound for its home port of Callao, lost her captain and three crewmen in a southeast gale off Cape

Flattery. She was severely damaged and blown up the coast to Nootka Sound where the anchor was dropped and repairs were made. Word of the *Florencia's* misfortune reached Victoria and the gunboat *Forward* was dispatched to assist. The disabled brigantine was taken in tow but the *Forward* developed engine trouble, cut the *Florencia* adrift and the two ships lost sight of each other in the darkness. After eight more days she was anchored near Ucluelet but eventually grounded in the cove on the islet. Her crew was rescued by the H.M.S. *Hecate* and taken to Victoria.

Half Moon Bay Trail

Half Moon Bay is a small, crescent-shaped cove south of Florencia Bay. The 500-metre trail crosses a headland between the two bays. It branches off the Willowbrae Trail a short distance before the descent to Florencia Bay. Like the Willowbrae Trail, the

Half Moon Bay Trail

Half Moon Bay Trail is extremely steep near the end but a good, winding boardwalk with handrails is there to help the hiker. As the boardwalk climbs down to the beach it makes a turn of nearly 180 degrees. A bench for pooped hikers sits on a landing about halfway down.

The boardwalk passes through a swampy area with an abundance of skunk cabbage, sword fern and salal before beginning its steep descent. As it winds toward the beach it passes beneath a huge coniferous snag with clumps of bracket fungus clinging to the trunk. They resemble old toads' heads, mounted like trophies on the sides of the tree.

The beach is a spot where chances of finding some solitude are good. Salmon fishermen occasionally spin-cast off the rocks at Wya Point, at the southwest end of the beach. Large numbers of California sea lions often haul out in winter on an islet which is visible from Wya Point.

Tofino's Tonquin Park

To reach this little local park, drive into Tofino on the main road, turn left on First Street and follow the road to a small parking area at the end. A three-minute walk through a pretty forest leads to a sandy beach, or you can cross "Alfred's Bridge" and walk another two minutes to some picnic tables on a grassy spot at the end of the trail.

Tonquin Park bears the name of an American ship which met a disastrous but deliberate end in 1811 when she exploded and sank near Echachis Island. She's been the subject of numerous unsuccessful searches by underwater archeologists.

Reports of how or where the *Tonquin* met her fate vary widely but modern research suggests she was blown up by a lone crewman, the ship's clerk, who put a torch to the vessel's powder magazine. The ship, according to the story, was anchored in Templar Channel and crewmen beckoned nearby Indians aboard. When they arrived the sailors were rude and abusive and even pushed some chieftains overboard. The Indians returned the following day, dugouts laden with furs to give the impression they'd returned on a friendly trading mission. There was gunfire and several crewmen were killed before the natives left.

Four crewmen escaped in a boat during the night and the severely injured clerk remained aboard. When the Indians returned the next morning the ship appeared abandoned. But as they climbed aboard, the clerk detonated the gunpowder, taking his own life along with many of the natives'. The four other crew members were apparently captured and fatally tortured.

A beach in Tonquin Park looks toward Templar Channel where the carnage occurred.

Ucluelet's He-Tin-Kis Park

This local park is a maze of trails beginning from a wooded parking area on the west side of Ucluth Peninsula Road, a short distance before Coast Guard Drive if you're headed toward Amphitrite Point.

A boardwalk from the parking lot makes an easy two or three-minute hike to a west-facing beach where a steep stairway climbs to the top of a headland. A trail to the right at the top of the stairs leads through the forest to some cliffs overlooking a tiny cove with a gravel and sand beach. To get to the beach stay on the trails to the right: don't go near the cliff edges. There are lots of exposed tree roots which are slippery in wet weather.

If you continue along the main trail at the top of the stairs you'll eventually return to the parking lot on a loop. Several other trails branch off the main trail to various viewpoints over the open Pacific, good places for whale watching in spring.

LANDING LONG BEACH LUNKERS — INLETS AND OPEN SEAS

Anglers who stand on the beach and cast into the pounding surf at Long Beach get wet feet more often than they get fish. On rare lucky days they catch salmon but usually, if they land anything, it's a lowly surf perch or flounder. Diligent anglers, however, do reasonably well casting from rock headlands, such as Wya or Portland points. Some land sizable spring salmon, many take the odd cod. The best shore casters attribute their success to practice, hours of watching conditions, and learning how to work the lures. It's a highly specialized form of fishing but extremely exciting for those who've mastered the techniques.

Methods for catching the elusive west coast salmon vary with the conditions and anglers' preferences. The best advice will always come from local anglers who've been out in the past day or two. Ask around before heading out. In the more sheltered waters of Tofino and Ucluelet inlets there's good sea-run cutthroat fishing near the mouths of creeks. Fish them with a fly or spinner on an incoming tide during periods of low light.

You need a boat to get to the most heavily-fished areas around Tofino and Ucluelet. If you don't have your own you may be able to rent one or charter one with a guide: check at local tourist bureaus, at government wharves, marinas and in local publications. Federal fishing licences are required to fish all "fin fish." Licences are available from some guides, the Fisheries and Oceans office in Tofino, the Ucluelet municipal office and most

Pacific Rim fishing

places which sell fishing tackle. Fishing regulations, published annually by the Department of Fisheries and Oceans, can usually be picked up, free of charge, at the same outlets. Changes made to the regulations after they've been published should be displayed in the Tofino and Ucluelet post offices or occasionally at government wharves.

Anglers fishing out of Tofino or Ucluelet need tide tables for Tofino as well as a compass and hydrographic charts for each area, described in the following sections. Charts and tide tables are available in local stores and marinas or can be ordered by mail. Prepayment is required for mail order purchases and catalogues and price lists are available free by writing to the addresses shown on p. 177. Fog, numerous reefs, strong tidal streams, heavy swells and unexpected squalls are the hazards here.

Tofino and Clayoquot Sound

Boats can be launched on paved ramps at Grice Bay or near the government wharf in Tofino. Hydrographic chart 3640, *Clayoquot Sound, Lennard Island to Estevan Point*, at a scale of 1:77,511, provides an overview of the area. For more detail use two charts — 3649 entitled *Clayoquot Sound, Southeast Portion*, at a scale of 1:40,000, and 3648 entitled *Clayoquot Sound, Northwest Portion*, at a scale of 1:36,488. For detail on Hayden Passage, Tsapee Narrows and Dawley Passage use 3643, *Plans in Clayoquot Sound*, at a scale of 1:18,280.

If you head northwest out of Tofino you can begin what is essentially a circumnavigation of Vargas Island. Run around the sand spit on the north side of Stubbs Island into Father Charles Channel, watching for rocks. From Moser Point, north through Father Charles Channel and along the shore of Vargas Island into Calmus Passage there's good chinook and coho fishing through summer. Bucktailing for cohoes is particularly good in September and early October. Jigging over Elbow Bank in Maurus Channel is generally productive although dogfish are a problem. On the western side of Vargas Island, Brabant Channel offers some reasonable summer fishing, but you're exposed here to the open Pacific so keep an eye on the weather. North of Brabant Channel big cohoes move into Russell Channel in late summer and early fall, making it excellent bucktailing water. Ling cod, chinook and rockfish are often taken after a flood tide in Hayden Pass at the north end of Millar Channel where tides run up to four knots.

On the opposite side of Tofino, to the east and northeast, the waters are more sheltered but not quite as productive. Chinook and coho salmon in Browning Passage are generally small through summer but big cohoes arrive in early fall. It's rocky in the pass and easier to drift fish than troll. Small boaters should be wary of tidal currents, up to five knots, between Riley and Morpheus Islands at the northwest end of Browning Passage. Tides here flood south and ebb north. Tides in Tsapee Narrows run up to four knots, flooding to the east, ebbing to the west. The currents produce some of the hottest year-round salmon fishing in the area with the runs peaking in July and August. Up the eastern side of Meares Island there's good chinook and cod fishing, particularly in summer. At the north end of Fortune Channel, Matlset Narrows gives up a few chinooks in summer. Currents in the narrows run up to four knots on spring tides.

Ucluelet and Western Barkley Sound

Few anglers fish Ucluelet Inlet but fishing is big business in Barkley Sound. There are several guide and charter outfits working out of Ucluelet. Check local publications and tourist information centres. There are paved boat ramps at Ucluelet's float plane base and at Bay Shore Marina. Three hydrographic charts are useful to fishermen in this area. An overview is given by 3671, *Barkley Sound*. Details of Ucluelet Inlet, at a scale of 1:15,000 are provided on 3646, *Plans in Barkley Sound*. Forbes Island, Toquart Bay, Lyall Point and all of the Broken Islands are shown in detail on 3670, *Broken Group*. Winds often funnel up Loudoun Channel, whipping the waves into whitecaps on the western side of Barkley Sound. Fog, especially in fall, is also a hazard to watch for.

Winter chinook fishing is good out of Ucluelet and big fish show from early spring to late summer. Some big cohoes arrive in June and stay for a short time and fishing for smaller cohoes is good in August and September. Generally, fishing along the entire western shore of Barkley Sound can be productive, although some places are fished more heavily than others.

Immediately outside Ucluelet Inlet is Carolina Channel, where small chinooks linger from late spring to mid-summer. Cohoes also show here from late spring to early fall and both coho and chinook salmon can be taken by trollers and drift fishermen. Similar methods are used at Amphitrite Point. Fishermen drifting off the lighthouse should beware of heavy surf that could chuck a small boat onto the rocks. Also near the approaches to Ucluelet Inlet, the Chrow Islands are a good trolling spot for chinooks from late spring to mid-summer.

Farther up the western side of Barkley Sound, Forbes Island gives up sizable salmon and ling cod for patient drift fishermen. Lyall Point is good mooching territory from spring until fall for chinook and ling fishermen. Toquart Bay, headquarters for many Barkley Sound fishermen, produces chinooks all summer and cohoes in late summer and early fall. Boats can be launched off the hard sand beach at Toquart Bay.

PACIFIC RIM PADDLING

The intricate waterways around Long Beach present a challenge for both expert and novice paddlers. Grice Bay, a large and shallow wildlife refuge within Pacific Rim Park, is ideal for beginners or families with young children. Beyond Tofino and the entrance to Clayoquot Sound, Hot Springs Cove beckons those capable of navigating through choppy seas and open ocean swells. Inland, a voyage down the lower Kennedy River is hampered only by one set of rapids. Adventuresome kayakers launch into the pounding surf at Long Beach or Wickaninnish to ride the crests back to shore.

Boat rental outlets come and go but canoes and kayaks may be available for hire: ask at the park information centre or at local tourist bureaus. Tide tables for Tofino are needed for the three trips outlined here. If you're paddling between late April and the end of October, when Daylight Saving Time is in effect, remember to add an hour to the times shown on the tables. Hydrographic charts and topographic maps, described under each heading, should be carried. Both the tide tables and charts are available in local stores and marinas. They can also be ordered by mail. Prepayment is required for mail order purchases of federal hydrographic charts and provincial topographic maps. Catalogues and price lists are available free by writing to the addresses shown on p. 177. Tide tables can also be ordered from the same address shown for hydrographic charts.

Grice Bay — Wildlife and Easy Water

Grice Bay is easy canoeing water for paddlers who prefer loafing in the sun to exercising their biceps. Hazards are minimal and chances of seeing harbor seals, porpoises and numerous birds are good.

The provincial topographic map 92F/4, entitled *Tofino*, is the best one for canoeing this area. It also shows Tofino Inlet, Meares Island and the village of Tofino. The same map can be used for a canoe trip from Kennedy Lake, down the lower Kennedy River to Tofino Inlet. The scale is 1:50,000.

The mudflats at Grice Bay are an important stopover for thousands of waterfowl migrating on the Pacific flyway. From October to December as many as 3,000 Canada geese may use the flats and about 500 may stay through winter. Fifty or 75 of Vancouver Island's 2,000-odd wintering trumpeter swans frequent the flats and, during winter, it's common to see up to 16,000 ducks — mallards, pintails, widgeon, mergansers, buffleheads, goldeneyes and others. Knobby-kneed great blue herons stalk the shallows and bald eagles feast on unwary waterfowl. Sometimes

Grice Bay

park naturalists conduct guided canoe trips at Grice Bay during summer: check at the information centre in the park.

The few dangers to canoeists or kayakers are fog, winds funneling up the centre of the bay, shallow waters and strong tidal currents in Tsapee Narrows, slightly more than one kilometre northwest of the park boundary. Tides in the narrows run up to four knots, flooding to the east, ebbing to the west. If you plan to venture beyond Grice Bay into Browning Passage, toward the village of Tofino, negotiate the narrows at slack tide.

Highlights here are Kootowis Falls, the marine life near Indian Island and several short, narrow fingers along the southern side of the bay. A paved boat ramp is located at the end of a 2.2 kilometre road from Highway 4.

Kennedy River — Slow-Moving Route to the Sea

With the exception of Kennfalls Rapids, an eight-kilometre trip down the tranquil lower Kennedy River is free of obstructions. There's good cutthroat trout fishing under the bridge where Kennedy Lake flows into the river and otters are commonly seen splashing among the lily pads in a large backwater two kilometres downstream from the bridge. The river is outside the park and there's no organized camping.

Use provincial topographic map 92F/4 entitled *Tofino*, at a scale of 1:50,000 for this trip.

To reach a launching point, drive on Highway 4 towards Port Alberni from the Ucluelet-Tofino-Alberni junction. After just over a kilometre turn left on MacMillan Bloedel's West Main. It's a restricted logging road and may not be open to the public during operating hours. Watch for signs. Slightly more than 11 kilometres along the road, cross the bridge over the top of the Kennedy River and stop at a nice, but small, camping spot on the shores of Kennedy Lake.

The campsite sits on a kilometre-wide peninsula between the Kennedy River bridge and another bridge which spans the entrance to Kennedy Lake's Clayoquot Arm. The arm is 11 kilometres long and nearly 2 kilometres wide; although some paddlers explore it, there are better places for small boats in the Long Beach area. Kennedy Lake is surrounded by steep-sided mountains and winds whip up Clayoquot Arm and across the main part of the lake with little warning. It is not only Vancouver Island's largest body of fresh water, but many believe it's the nastiest.

You can launch near the Kennedy River bridge and paddle the slow-moving stream for six kilometres before reaching the rapids. The river is about 50 metres wide for the first two kilometres. Beyond the first backwater it widens to about 100 metres for another two kilometres before opening to what looks like a lake. It then bends to the northeast and narrows to about 25 metres before rounding a point. A turn to the southeast takes you into another pretty backwater where a logging road near the shore can be used as a portage trail around Kennfalls Rapids.

These rapids are a kilometre upstream from tidewater at Tofino Inlet and you're nuts if you try and paddle through them. A canoeist who tried in 1971 didn't make it. Pull out in the backwater about 400 metres upstream from the rapids and pack your boat nearly a kilometre along the old road, then about 200 metres down a steep hill to a point below the rapids. Some of the portage is rough going but at least it's tolerably short.

The river drains into Kennedy Cove where you can turn toward the west and hug the shore of Tofino Inlet down to Indian Bay, through a narrow channel and across the mouth of Grice Bay to the boat ramp in Pacific Rim Park, a total of 11 kilometres.

Tofino to Hot Springs Cove

A paddle from Tofino to Hot Springs Cove provides an intimate look at nearly every feature the southwest coast of Vancouver Island has to offer. Long, sandy beaches, craggy, exposed shorelines, seabirds, whales, virgin forests, wooded mountains,

Indian villages, shallow inlets and lagoons, open seas, sheltered channels and hot springs. But the hazards, depending on tides and weather, make this journey a trip only for experienced canoeists and kayakers. It shouldn't be tackled in an open canoe because conditions seldom remain ideal for the time needed to complete the trip.

Three federal hydrographic charts are helpful for this trip but you could get away with one. Chart 3640, entitled *Clayoquot Sound, Lennard Island to Estevan Point*, at a scale of 1:77,511 provides an overview of the entire area. For more detail use two charts — 3649 entitled *Clayoquot Sound, Southeast Portion*, at a scale of 1:40,000 and 3648 entitled *Clayoquot Sound, Northwest Portion*, at a scale of 1:36,488.

Though there are creeks on some of the islands along the route, it's wise to carry fresh water as it's not always available. You can launch from Tofino's government wharf or from nearby beaches. The distance between Tofino and Hot Springs Cove, as the crow flies, is 37 kilometres. The most direct water route is about 40 kilometres but other routes could be considerably longer.

The tiny town of Tofino is dominated by Meares Island, an 8,600-hectare wilderness with mountain peaks rising nearly 800 metres above the sea. The island is larger than Hong Kong or Bermuda but inhabited by only 200 Clayoquot Indians, in the village of Opitsat on the southwest end. Their reserve encompasses 70 hectares but they utilize all of the shores and woodlands, as their ancestors have for more than 4,000 years. They harvest fur from traplines laid generations ago, net chum and coho salmon from myriad creeks, and hunt blacktail deer that seek sanctuary in stands of centuries-old cedar and hemlock. A midden at Opitsat, one of 190 archeological sites on the island, is five metres deep.

Among the island's most intriguing areas is Lemmens Inlet, which almost bisects the island. Its lagoons and mudflats are an important stopover and wintering area for migratory birds. Eelgrass in the inlet is perfect habitat for big Dungeness crabs. A growing number of oyster and salmon farmers have been setting up operations in the inlet.

Paddlers who begin their voyage to Hot Springs Cove with a side trip to Meares Island should be wary of tidal currents, up to five knots, between Riley and Morpheus Islands at the northwest end of Browning Passage near the entrance to Lemmens Inlet. Tides here flood south and ebb north.

Nearly six kilometres north of Morpheus Island on the eastern side of Lemmens Inlet is Adventure Cove, where an American trader named Captain Robert Gray spent the fall and winter of 1791 and '92 building a small sloop. A two-storey log house was erected and named Fort Defiance, to be guarded against Indian attacks by Gray's crew of 50 men. The exact location of Fort Defiance remained a mystery for more than 170 years, until 1966 when it was discovered by some Tofino residents. The provincial government later officially declared it an historic site.

Paddlers leaving Tofino for Hot Springs Cove should beware of tides up to three knots in Duffin Passage, between Stubbs and Felice Islands. The long sand spit on the north end of Stubbs Island is an ideal picnic spot, now that the impaled heads have gone. For several years after a fierce battle between warring Indians in 1855, passing mariners were greeted by the heads of 18 casualties, mounted on sticks and spread along the spit. Today there's a lodge on the island, a good place for a lavish dinner.

Vargas Island, west of Stubbs, is almost flat compared with the other islands surrounding Tofino. The surf on the southern side of the island can be dangerous and if weather is less than excellent the safest route toward Hot Springs Cove is up Father Charles Channel and around the top of Vargas via Calmus Passage. There are several nice beaches on the island on both the east and west sides.

Flores Island, northwest of Vargas, is inhabited by about 400 Indians at Ahousat, in Matilda Inlet on the southeast side. There's a store and post office in the village. This area is also the site of Gibson Marine Park, a 142-hectare chunk of public land with a beautiful sand beach and lukewarm hot springs. The springs flow 11 litres a minute at a temperature of 25 degrees Celsius, half as warm as the springs at Hot Springs Cove. They run into a concrete pool measuring about 2.4 metres wide by 6 metres long and 1.2 metres deep. An 800-metre trail from Matilda Inlet follows an old hydro line to the springs. Another trail leads to the southern, exposed side of the island where there's good camping on the beach at Whitesand Cove.

The beaches around Flores Island are long and numerous, pleasant places to relax and watch passing gray whales or sluggish basking sharks, some as long as 12 metres, lying tranquilly on the surface with their dorsal fins exposed. Like Vargas Island, the south side of Flores Island is exposed to the open Pacific and should be traveled only by experienced paddlers. The safer, but much longer route, is up Millar Channel and through Hayden Pass, where tides run up to four knots, into Shelter Inlet. You can then paddle along the north side of Flores Island, across Sydney Inlet and around Sharp Point into Hot Springs Cove. Old charts may show the cove as Refuge Cove, a name which was changed to avoid confusion with another cove of the same name elsewhere on the B.C. coast.

The hot springs, near the tip of Openit Peninsula on the eastern side of the cove, look much like a typical west coast creek. The surf usually makes landing directly in front of the springs difficult: it's preferable to paddle farther into the cove and pull out at a government wharf. From there it's an easy half-hour hike to the springs.

HOT SPRINGS SOOTHE ACHING BONES

Vancouver Island's only known hot springs flow a total of 45 metres from the source, at a rate of 450 litres a minute, over a waterfall and through a series of pools to the sea. They look much like any other west coast creek but the water is 50 degrees Celsius.

The hot springs, 37 kilometres northwest of Tofino, make an unforgettable day-trip for people visiting Long Beach. They're particularly refreshing in a mid-winter downpour, a good place to usher in a new year if you happen to be holed up in a seaside cabin for the festive season.

Hot Springs Cove, named for the springs, is accessible only by float plane or boat. Pacific Rim Airlines runs scheduled flights twice a day between Hot Springs Cove and Tofino and there are rarely more than four or five days a year when planes are grounded by bad weather. A one-way flight is about 20 minutes. Local boat owners often run charters to the cove or offer nature tours which include the hot springs: check advertisements in local publications or ask at tourist information outlets.

The flight from Tofino provides aerial views of Vancouver Island's western mountains and forests, long sandy beaches, remote Indian settlements, sea lion haulouts and seabird colonies. More than 14,000 birds nest on Cleland Island and Plover Reefs, near the entrance to Brabant Channel, which you may pass en route to the cove. Plover Reefs are also a winter haulout for more than 200 Steller's sea lions. Gray whales, humpbacks and killer whales are frequently seen on the flight to the hot springs.

Planes and boats dock at a government wharf in the cove, site of a once-thriving fuel and supply business for west coast fishermen. Derelict buildings, weatherbeaten walkways and other relics at the head of the wharf mark the start of a two-kilometre trail and boardwalk to the springs. A general store has been open year-round recently near the government dock to provide for transient boaters and fishermen.

The hot springs are a part of Maquinna Provincial Park, a 12-hectare undeveloped tract of public land near the southern tip of Openit Peninsula. Camping is allowed in the park and local Indians have opened a campground near the springs.

Several Indians live at Hot Springs Cove and it can be a bustling refuge during fishing seasons. Summer visitors can lounge in a steaming pool and watch fishboats chugging in and out of the cove. During winter, however, the springs are deserted on many days.

The route to the springs is a pleasant half-hour stroll through a rain forest and over rocky hills above the cove. The scent of sulphur and steam rising above the salal underbrush draws hikers to the pools. The pools above a three-metre waterfall are usually cool enough for bathing only in winter, when cold runoff mixes with the mineral water.

Outdoor shower at Hot Springs Cove

Half a dozen rocky pools, each less than a metre deep, run in a series down to the ocean, becoming successively cooler as they approach the sea. If the tide is high or seas are rough, a bather can stand under a wall of frigid seawater as the surf funnels up a gulch into the lower pools. Others are content to loll in the higher, hotter pools, sipping something cool while breakers crash against the surrounding shores. Most bathers wear only old sneakers, leaving clothes and wet-weather gear nearby in plastic bags to protect them from heavy rains.

Many west coasters believe the sulphur, mineral salts, iron oxides and calcium in the springs bring good health to those who drink from the pools and soak in the steaming water. People who suffer from rheumatism or arthritis have reportedly made annual pilgrimages to Hot Springs Cove for several years to soak their creaking bones in the healthful mineral water.

AFTER LONG BEACH, WHAT NEXT?

It would seem impossible that any place could match the exceptional ocean scenery of Long Beach. But what about the intricate waterways in the Broken Group Islands of Barkley Sound? What about the deep ravines, rushing streams and waterfalls of the West Coast Trail? It's pointless to try and compare these places to one another: they're equally beautiful, equally distinctive. If you're impressed with one, you should explore the others.

CHAPTER THREE

Barkley Sound
A HERITAGE
TO USE AND PRESERVE

B arkley Sound, between Long Beach and the West Coast
Trail, encompasses nearly 800 square kilometres, with To-
quart Bay and Rainy Bay in the north, and Cape Beale and
Amphitrite Point in the south, where the sound faces the Pacific
Ocean. The villages of Bamfield and Ucluelet, on opposite sides of
Barkley Sound, are only 30 kilometres apart, yet their residents as-
sociate with one another infrequently.

Hundreds of untamed islands and islets lie in clusters across
the sound, separated by wide, windswept channels. Long, narrow inlets penetrate the forested mountains around the edges of
the sound, slicing into a remote and rugged landscape. These inlets, and the bays and harbors amid the islands provide shelter for

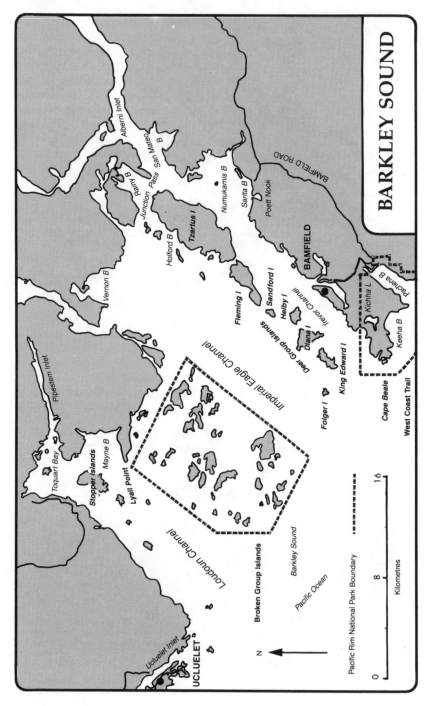

BARKLEY SOUND

boaters and fishermen who come to explore the intricate water-ways and reap the harvests of the surrounding seas.

In the middle of the sound the hundred-odd islands and is-lets of the Broken Group are a sheltered haven for canoeists and kayakers. Across the often treacherous waters of Imperial Eagle and Trevor channels, Bamfield is a bustling centre for fishermen, scuba divers, kayakers and sightseers. It's a starting point for hikes to Cape Beale, and Tapaltos and Keeha bays. And it's the northwest end of the West Coast Trail, a place to rest after a tiring hike along the isolated shores of southwest Vancouver Island.

Bamfield, Toquart Bay and Ucluelet are base camps for hun-dreds of sport fishermen who search the waters of Barkley Sound for chinook and coho salmon. It's the salmon fishing capital of Canada and anglers come from around the world for the enviable privilege of landing trophy-sized fish. The fishermen and others who travel Barkley Sound cross the paths of migrating gray whales, pods of killer whales and porpoises. Harbor seals, and Calfornia and Steller's sea lions seek the same salmon as the fishermen. Barkley Sound is endowed with one of the highest concentrations of bald eagles in North America: probably 100 pairs build lofty stick nests in the crowns of towering evergreens around Pacific Rim. And like the seals, the sea lions and the fisher-men, the eagles scan the waters of the sound for the silvery sal-mon.

Bamfield fishermen maintain their nets

The mouth of Barkley Sound is so wide that before the days of modern navigation ships would mistake it for the entrance to Juan de Fuca Strait. They'd crash onto the rocks along the outer edge of the sound, to be buried beneath the swells on this stretch of coast aptly named the Graveyard of the Pacific. Some of these unfortunate vessels have become major attractions for scuba divers, another feature to bolster the burgeoning tourist industry of Barkley Sound.

There are changes happening here. Pacific Rim National Park, with its islands in the Broken Group and its West Coast Trail between Pachena Bay and Port Renfrew, has drawn attention from the outside world to a once-isolated sanctum known only to a handful of Vancouver Islanders. While some locals resent the intrusion, others recognize the salability of the scenery that's been a natural part of their lives for so many years, so many generations. Although they may disagree on the need to develop a tourist industry, most agree on at least one thing: the challenge now is to keep this magnificent corner of Canada as it's always been.

TO BARKLEY SOUND BY LAND, SEA OR AIR

Bamfield is the main population centre on the eastern side of Barkley Sound. It's accessible by gravel logging roads from Port Alberni and Youbou, a village on the north side of Cowichan Lake. These two roads meet at Franklin River Camp where a single road continues to Bamfield. Total distance from Port Alberni to Bamfield is 102 kilometres. From Youbou it's 108 kilometres. Youbou can be reached by taking the Lake Cowichan turnoff from Highway 1, about 3 kilometres north of the city of Duncan.

Both roads are maintained according to use by forest companies which keep them open. On rare occasions the road from Youbou is closed due to extreme fire hazards. Otherwise the roads are open to the public year-round. Although often dotted with potholes and bumps, they are passable for ordinary vehicles. They can be used at any time of day or week but logging trucks always have the right-of-way.

Boaters who want to avoid the logging roads often launch at Port Alberni and run nearly 60 kilometres down Alberni Inlet and Trevor Channel to Bamfield Inlet.

The opposite side of Barkley Sound can be reached by boat from Ucluelet or Toquart Bay. To find Toquart Bay, drive slightly more than 85 kilometres on Highway 4 from Port Alberni toward Long Beach. As the highway skirts Kennedy Lake watch for a gravel logging road running parallel to the highway, on the opposite side from the lake. It's a rough 16-kilometre drive to Toquart Bay where boats can be launched from the beach.

The *Lady Rose*, a 31-metre cargo and passenger ship, makes several trips a week, year-round, between Port Alberni and Bamfield. She's used regularly by Bamfielders and West Coast Trail hikers. The ship also makes summer runs through the Broken Group Islands to Ucluelet.

Pacific Rim Airlines, based in Port Alberni, has scheduled flights to Bamfield and Ucluelet and can be chartered to various places on the west coast.

THE LADY ROSE

Since 1960 the *Lady Rose* has continuously graced the waters of Barkley Sound. Painted the colors of a killer whale, she chugs along at 11 knots, carrying passengers, mail and cargo to villages and way points around the sound. For some of the citizens of Bamfield, Ucluelet, Kildonan and smaller coastal camps she's the primary link with the outside world.

Based at Alberni Harbor Quay, the *Lady Rose* is a 31-metre, 199-ton packet freighter. She has a beam of 7 metres, draws more than 2 metres and is powered by a 385-horsepower Caterpillar diesel.

She can carry 100 passengers and during summer as many as 12,000 may take the run between Port Alberni and Ucluelet. Equipped with cameras, warm windbreakers and binoculars,

Lady Rose *leaving Bamfield*

they board at Port Alberni first thing in the morning for a 10-hour return cruise down Alberni Inlet, through the Broken Group Islands and into Ucluelet. The ship stops for an hour and a half before returning to Port Alberni, a total return distance of about 160 kilometres. Some passengers travel one way, disembarking at Ucluelet to spend a few days at Long Beach before boarding a bus for a tour through the Mackenzie Mountains back to Port Alberni.

Nearly two dozen canoes and kayaks with camping gear can be loaded in the hold and ferried to a float at Gibraltar Island, where the Lady Rose drops off and picks up paddlers from late spring to early fall. The ship is also gaining popularity among bicyclists. Some camp a while at Long Beach, then cruise back to Port Alberni; others cycle out of Long Beach through the mountains.

The *Lady Rose* travels between Port Alberni and Bamfield several times a week throughout the year. For many Bamfielders, the ship is a marine bus service, reliable transportation to paved highways that spares them a long and lumpy ride over gravel logging roads to the cities of Vancouver Island. She's also a vital delivery ship for inhabitants of logging and fish camps, or private homes on islands and along the Vancouver Island coastline. She packs in virtually anything -- antiques, fuel, furniture, industrial equipment, livestock, food, pianos, whatever's needed. During summer she carries hikers traveling to and from the West Coast Trail.

Alberni Inlet, the longest on Vancouver Island, rivals the scenic fjords of Norway. Flanked by wooded peaks up to 1,300 metres high, the inlet stretches 40 kilometres from the mouth of the Somass River to the entrance to Barkley Sound near San Mateo Bay. The width of the inlet rarely exceeds a kilometre and more than five dozen creeks drain the surrounding mountains. The inlet is internationally known for its abundance of coho and chinook salmon and passengers aboard the *Lady Rose* often see them jumping. Bald eagles are occasionally seen swooping down to pluck unsuspecting fish from the surface. In winter and spring, sea lions are a common sight and once in a while a pod of killer whales passes the ship or a black bear wanders onto an isolated beach.

Passengers can pull up a deck chair or ensconce themselves on a bench on the aft deck to take in the scenery as the ship steams along the inlet. Down below there are home-cooked meals and a small lounge, spartan but warm.

The steel-hulled vessel was built in 1937 in Glasgow, Scotland for the Union Steamship Company of Vancouver, to be used in Howe Sound on B.C.'s lower mainland. She arrived through the Panama Canal and, in 1942, joined the fleet operated by the Royal Canadian Army Service Corps. She carried armed forces personnel, mail and food between Port Alberni and Ucluelet for about 7,000 servicemen. After reconditioning, she returned to Howe Sound for Union Steamships in 1946, before being sold in 1950 to Harbor Navigation Company of Vancouver. Coast Ferries Limited chartered her in 1954 for service between Steveston, on the lower Fraser River, and the Gulf Islands. After a short stint in the Alert Bay area of northern Vancouver Island she returned to Port Alberni in 1960.

The *Lady Rose* now is operated by Alberni Marine Transportation Incorporated. Reservations, preferably a month in advance, are required for canoes and kayaks and it's wise for passengers to make reservations if traveling in summer. Schedule, fare and other information about this heritage vessel is available from the address on p. 177.

INFORMATION — HELPFUL ADVICE FOR NEWCOMERS

Bamfield is so small that you can often find tourist information by asking someone on the street or at a store. The tiny town, however, does have a chamber of commerce which operates a tourist information centre in the "downtown" area. Information on accommodation, camping, fishing and diving charters, nature cruises, boat and canoe rentals, water taxis, tourist attractions and services, transportation, restaurants, local events and other topics is available.

Information on Bamfield and other parts of Barkley Sound is also available from the Pacific Rim Tourist Association in Port Alberni. Parks Canada, with information centres at Long Beach and Pachena Bay, can provide detail on the West Coast Trail, Barkley Sound's Broken Group Islands and areas outside Pacific Rim National Park. For addresses of tourist information outlets see p. 177.

Local businesses advertise in the *Barkley Sounder*, a monthly journal published in Bamfield. It's an excellent source of information on subjects ranging from community issues, weather and real estate to history, profiles and opinions. It's well worth the price of a copy.

ACCOMMODATION AND CAMPING

For a village of slightly more than 200, Bamfield has a surprising array of accommodation. Motels, lodges, fishing resorts and campgrounds are available in and around the town. Some of the newer establishments are aimed mainly at attracting sport fishermen. They offer boat rentals or charters, guide services, tackle and a variety of package deals. Other accommodation owners can provide an entire lodge, with kitchen facilities, for large groups of fishermen, scuba divers, hikers and general loafers. As Bamfield's main street is an inlet, most lodges or resorts provide dock space.

The B.C. Ministry of Tourism's *Accommodation Guide* is a good source for accommodation information, including detail on commercial campgrounds. Other accommodation information may be available from local tourist bureaus.

Campers who want to drive directly to a campsite can set up at Pachena Bay, about five kilometres by road from Bamfield. The Ohiaht Indian band operates a campground, store, coffee shop, gas station and tire repair shop on the Anacla Reserve. Outhouses and water from taps are provided and camping fees are charged. The sites are set among tall trees above Pachena Beach, a striking one-kilometre stretch of sand facing the open Pacific. The Pachena River meanders down from Pachena Lake, forming the northwest border of the beach. This campground is easily accessible by road and it's wise to lock food and valuables in a car when leaving the campsite or going to bed. Ice chests, stoves, fishing tackle and other items have been known to disappear.

Pacific Rim Park's West Coast Trail information centre, an A-framed cabin, sits in a field adjoining the Indians' campground. A parking lot is provided and camping is allowed here for up to three nights. Camping here, however, is mainly for hikers walking the West Coast Trail.

Bamfield's Centennial Park, a camping area next to the boat ramp and government wharf at Port Désiré, is a handy spot for anglers who want quick access to the fishy waters of Barkley Sound. Parking spaces are set aside for vehicles and boat trailers and daily fees are charged for both parking and camping. Water and outhouses are provided and fires are allowed in established fire pits. Check also for a commercial campground near the boat ramp at Port Désiré.

Three of the the the beaches described in this chapter's hiking section — Brady's Beach, Tapaltos Bay and Keeha Beach — are excellent campsites. A boat is needed to get to the heads of the trails; if you take a water taxi make sure to arrange for a ride back. A creek from Kichha Lake runs down to the southeast end of Keeha Beach, but water should be packed in by campers at Brady's Beach and Tapaltos Bay.

Camping in the Deer Group Islands, outside the entrance to Bamfield Inlet, is popular among canoeists, kayakers and other boaters. If you don't have your own boat you can catch a water taxi. Some boat rental outlets or charter boat operators will take campers and gear to the islands and leave them with a radio for as long as they like. When they want to return they call on the radio for a ride. Kayaks, canoes and motorized boats are available for rent in Bamfield.

There's plenty of driftwood for campfires on these beaches. Deadfalls or standing trees should not be taken from surrounding forests. Fires should be lit below the winter high-tide mark and thoroughly extinguished before going to bed or leaving the campsite.

BAMFIELD — BOATS AND BUSTLE

You can lean against the rail on Bamfield's boardwalk and watch a stream of boats flow past the shops and houses that overlook the inlet: fishboats, sailboats, rowboats, lifeboats, speedboats, scows, kayaks, canoes, inflatables, cargo carriers, passenger vessels, dinghies and dories. There's a constant hum of diesel engines and outboard motors as the parade of vessels up and down the inlet carries on through the day. Bamfield Inlet is this little unincorporated village's main street and without a boat you don't get far.

The inlet, about four kilometres long by 250 metres wide, divides the tiny town in two: Bamfield East was connected to the outside word in 1963 when a road was built to join logging roads leading to Vancouver Island cities. Across the inlet, Bamfield

Bamfield

West sits on the northern end of Mills Peninsula, accessible only by boat. Most of the homes, businesses, government wharves, bustle and activity are centred around the top half of the inlet. For a town of just over 200 people, and a summer population that swells to about 1,000, the services are surprising. They include motels, lodges and cottages, general stores, a post office, a Canadian Coast Guard station, bait and fishing supplies, a machine shop, outpost hospital, school, cafes and restaurants, campgrounds and fish processors. There's no bank or liquor store.

Bamfield boardwalk

For newcomers, the boardwalk along the shores of Bamfield West is among the town's most attractive features. It clings to a rocky shore, stretching almost two kilometres from government wharves at either end. Neatly painted, wood-sided houses, vegetable and flower gardens line the boardwalk. Every house has a moorage float with a gangway connecting it to the boardwalk. Boathouses — floating garages — are tied to some floats and many are piled high with boat gear, nets, floats and other useful appurtenances.

At the north end, the Canadian Coast Guard station, with its trimmed lawns and bright white buildings, sits with its lifeboat ready to rush to the rescue of misfortunate mariners in Barkley Sound. On a hill above the station, the Bamfield Inn watches over its own fleet of high-speed boats, decked out with swivel seats to fish the salmon in comfort. Farther along, people gather at the general store and post office to discuss local events and issues.

Across the inlet, in Bamfield East, the gray concrete face of the Bamfield Marine Station looks across to the north end of the boardwalk. The station, established in the early 1970s, is a research and teaching centre for five western Canadian universities. The main building once housed the offices for operators who translated messages sent on the Trans-Pacific cable.

Bamfield, because of the inlet's soft floor and gently- sloping shoreline, was selected as the western North American terminus for the Trans-Pacific cable, at nearly 6,400 kilometres the longest submarine telegraph cable in the world. Part of a system of communications linking commonwealth countries, the cable ran from Bamfield to Fanning Island, a coral atoll in the middle of the Pacific Ocean near the equator. From there it connected to Australia.

From 1902 as many as 30 operators worked around the clock translating messages into telegraphic signals and relaying them across the world. In 1926 the cable was duplicated to provide faster service and the concrete building overlooking Bamfield Inlet was erected. But in 1959 a new cable office was built in Port Alberni and the Bamfield operations shut down. A few years later several houses, and an elegant old building resembling a luxury hotel, were demolished and the property was sold to the universities.

Behind the marine station, Grappler Inlet winds past Port Désiré more than two kilometres to a shallow lagoon. For Bamfielders, Port Désiré is the country, a tranquil refuge from the bustle and traffic around the corner in Bamfield Inlet. The pace is similar in Bamfield South, near the lower half of Bamfield Inlet. Here a few new houses are spaced between dilapidated shacks and weatherworn, abandoned fishboats, half buried on the muddy shores.

Bamfield belies the belief that Vancouver Island's isolated coastal communities are sleepy hideaways for slowpokes and hermits. It's the meeting place for outdoorsmen who come from everywhere for a taste of the Pacific coast. It's the gateway to Barkley Sound, where salmon fishermen test their skills and kayakers explore the intricate waterways of the Broken Group Islands. It's the northwest end of the famous West Coast Trail, a place to rest after a week in the bush, or a final glimpse of civilization before setting out. It's the starting point for hikes to lighthouses and beaches facing the open Pacific. It's shelter and supplies for sailors, yachtsmen and commercial fishermen traveling the west coast.

Such a prominent role for so tiny a town.

POLICE AND MEDICAL SERVICES

The Royal Canadian Mounted Police in Port Alberni enforce laws in Bamfield and Barkley Sound. They have a high-speed boat to get them to Toquart Bay, the Broken Group and the village of Bamfield if there's trouble brewing. They are also responsible for law enforcement at Pachena Bay and on the West Coast Trail. Parks Canada wardens help enforce laws within Pacific Rim National Park.

West Coast General Hospital is located in Port Alberni and Bamfield has its own medical clinic and Red Cross Outpost. If an emergency evacuation is required a helicopter usually carries out the patient. There is no pharmacy in Bamfield so people who need prescription drugs should bring enough for their stay in the Barkley Sound area.

BAMFIELD HIKING — RAIN FORESTS, BOATS AND BEACHES

When hikers think of Bamfield many automatically associate the little village with the West Coast Trail. But the West Coast Trail, which actually begins five kilometres out of town at Pachena Bay, is not the only hike originating from Bamfield. It is by far the longest, but there are also attractive day or overnight hikes to Tapaltos Bay, Keeha Bay, Cape Beale and Brady's Beach. All of these rain forest trails lead to sandy, surf-battered shores with striking views and acres of driftwood and logs.

You can drive to the start of the West Coast Trail, but the heads of the other trails can be reached only by boat. A canoe or rowboat will do, and water taxis are available in Bamfield. Some of

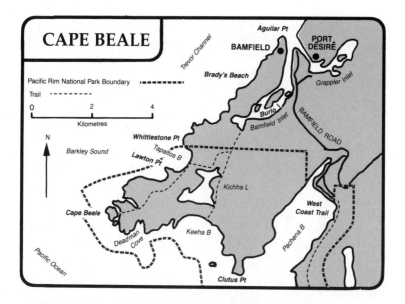

these hikes make good family outings, easy enough for a three-year-old or a baby in a backpack. Others are a misery for little children, or adults in sorry shape. Fresh water is available on some routes but it's wise to carry a litre or two of your own, along with lunch or at least a fair-sized snack. Boots are better than sneakers and rain gear should be carried if there's a cloud anywhere in the sky, particularly on the longer walks. Maps and compasses are unnecessary but they add interest to any hike. A provincial topographic map at a scale of 1:50,000, number 92C/14 entitled *Barkley Sound*, can be purchased from government agents throughout the province or mail ordered by writing to the address on p. 177. The general stores in Bamfield may carry maps.

People hiking to Brady's Beach, Tapaltos Bay or Cape Beale may wonder what produces the low-pitched sighing sound that reverberates across the surrounding seas. It sounds like a lovelorn bullfrog calling hopefully for a mate. It's actually a whistle buoy on Sea Pool Rocks, two kilometres northwest of Talpaltos Bay near the entrance to Trevor Channel. The action of the waves compresses air in the buoy and blows the horn, reminding passing ships that the rocks are nearby. It sounds similar to a foghorn, although it blows in all weather.

Pachena Bay to Pachena Point

The first 9 kilometres of the West Coast Trail, once a supply road to Pachena Lighthouse, are wide and easy, by comparison to the rest of the trail. Between 1907 and 1912 a team of 60 men,

107

using hand saws and horse-drawn equipment, carved a road through the wilderness between Bamfield and Pachena Point. When it became obvious that the construction of a road to Carmanah Point was impractical, a trail 1.5 metres wide was built instead. It's a good day hike through the woods from Pachena Bay with side paths running down to good camping beaches. It can be hiked at any time of year, but if you plan a winter walk of the entire 18 kilometres return, start early to get back before dark. There's a parking lot near the beginning of the trail.

Small youngsters can handle at least some of the walk. About 5.5 kilometres from the start a trail leads to a beach with good views out to Seabird Rocks, a nesting colony for about 2,000 seabirds. Another path runs down to a beach a kilometre farther along the West Coast Trail. Keep your nose peeled as you approach Pachena Point. About 700 metres before the lighthouse a viewpoint looks toward Flat Rocks, a winter haulout for Steller's sea lions. About 100 or 150 usually hang around the rocks in winter and early spring, but occasionally 400 or 500 may haul out for a few days at a time.

The meticulously maintained, white-sided, red-roofed buildings of Pachena Lighthouse, established in 1907, sit high above the rocky shores, surrounded by forests. There are views along nearby shores and across the mouth of Juan de Fuca Strait to Washington's Olympic Peninsula.

Brady's Beach

Brady's Beach is a local hideaway halfway up the western side of Mills Peninsula. Take a boat or water taxi to the government dock where the boardwalk along Bamfield West begins. Walk the trail above the dock up a short hill to a gravel road and

Brady's Beach

turn right. In a few moments you'll come to an intersection and it's a simple matter of following the signs. The walk is a pleasant half-hour stroll amid tall evergreens with salal, ivy and ferns growing along the edges of the trail.

The surf echoes through the trees as the trail approaches the beach. You'll step onto a beautiful sandy shore facing the Deer Group Islands near the entrance to Trevor Channel. Tall, weatherbeaten rocks with wind-worn trees clumped on the tops stand out on the beach. Mussels and starfish surround the tide pools and you can walk on the sand between barnacled boulders toward the headlands to the south. Harbor seals may bob about in the surf and fishboats chug up and down Trevor Channel as they travel in and out of Bamfield. Sometimes a chilly wind blows up the channel but there's plenty of driftwood to build a fire and fend off the cold.

Cape Beale and Tapaltos Bay

The six-kilometre trail from the head of Bamfield Inlet to Cape Beale was cleared in 1873 when the lighthouse was built. It was the only land link between the cape and village and in 1899 the same route was used to extend the Victoria-Cape Beale telegraph line to Bamfield. Though the trail has been modified over the years, the old single strand of galvanized wire, strung from tree to tree, is still visible along some stretches.

The Cape Beale headland generally refers to the large area between Pachena Bay and the cape. It's a part of Pacific Rim Park's West Coast Trail section and Parks Canada is expected to eventually improve the condition of the Cape Beale trail. By 1986, when the provincial and federal governments were still dickering over park boundaries, no trail maintenance had been done.

At one time the hike took about an hour and a half one way, but it could take an hour longer, depending on the condition of the trail. Bridges are rickety and bush is thick in places but the trail is clearly defined. Exposed roots are tangled across many sections and are slippery if it's been raining. Mud is also a nuisance. Wear good boots, long pants and pack drinking water. Eight and nine-year-old kids have been known to hike the trail but it's a bit rough for younger children.

The lighthouse is perched high on a rocky promontory, separated from surrounding lands by a shallow, sandy channel. You can walk across the channel at low tides but you have to swim it when the tide's in. Tide tables for Tofino should be consulted to plan your arrival at low tide, leaving enough time to explore the lighthouse grounds and get back across the channel before the tide floods. Remember to add an hour to the time shown on the tables if you're hiking while Daylight Saving Time is in effect.

Take a canoe, kayak, rowboat, water taxi or whatever else is available down Bamfield Inlet to the start of the trail, 2.5 kilometres from the government wharf in Bamfield East. Head for the mouth of a small creek on the southeast side of the basin at the head of the inlet. Surveyor's tape and old floats mark the beginning of the trail.

There's a fork in the trail, with a directional sign, about 20 minutes from the start. Take the right fork toward Tapaltos Bay and Cape Beale and within about five minutes there's another fork near a swamp. Keep to the right and when you reach the swamp follow markers to the right then walk left along an uprooted tree which crosses a bog. Trail markers lead the way on the other side of the bog.

En route to Cape Beale trail

Tapaltos Bay is about half an hour beyond the bog. It's a pretty, crescent-shaped beach stretching more than a kilometre between Lawton and Whittlestone points. Like Brady's Beach, Tapaltos Bay faces the Deer Group Islands near the entrance to Trevor Channel and is exposed to the pounding surf. The Tapaltos Bay Hilton, a ramshackle one-room shanty surrounded by encroaching underbrush and beachcombed treasures, has a commanding view of the sea from a hillside about 100 metres southwest of where the trail hits the beach. A driftwood archway, embellished by plastic bleach bottles, styrofoam floats, frayed nylon ropes, sea shells and other beach debris, covers the bottom of a wooden staircase leading to the shack.

Tapaltos Bay Hilton

The trail to Cape Beale, beyond the Tapaltos Bay Hilton, is marked by tape and old floats about 75 metres from the end of the beach. The terrain is up and down from here. After crossing the channel at low tide there's a steep climb up a paved walkway to the lighthouse.

Like others on the west coast, the lighthouse is a collection of tidy white buildings with bright red roofs. The lawns are trimmed like a golf course and the lightkeepers usually maintain an elaborate vegetable garden. The lightkeeper and assistant, with their families, collect rain water from the roofs of their houses and store it in reservoirs. One house fills a 90,000-litre reservoir, another fills 45,000 litres. Both overflow before December.

In the early years the only communication between Victoria and Cape Beale was an Indian messenger who took three days to paddle one way to Victoria. After the telegraph line was strung along the coast as far as Cape Beale in 1890, communications improved but storms and fallen trees frequently killed the line for months at a time, invariably at times it was needed most. Today, although Cape Beale appears isolated, there's a steady stream of visitors hiking the trail or boating in from Bamfield. The visitors' book is signed by people from around the world — Switzerland, England, New Zealand, the Philippines, Germany, Tanzania and other faraway places. The lightkeeper frequently goes to town and, if the weather's not too terrible, sport fishermen spend a lot of time drifting off the cape.

The light beams from a height of 53 metres above sea level, guiding ships toward the entrance to Juan de Fuca Strait. There is an unimpeded view of Pachena Light to the southeast and across Barkley Sound to Amphitrite Light near Ucluelet. But even with today's connections to the outside world and modern navigational equipment, Cape Beale remains a formidable natural hazard to ships that venture too close. Winds here have been recorded at 160 kilometres an hour: violent seas hammer at the reefs and rocky shores, spraying the glass around the top of the light tower. In this part of the Graveyard of the Pacific many ships lie buried beneath the seas.

One of the most dramatic rescues at Cape Beale was carried out on Feb. 28, 1976, when a fishboat with four men aboard was swept onto the rocks in the night. The lightkeeper had seen a boat rounding the cape and he thought it was too close. He later saw a spotlight flashing through the sky. Seas were high and snow was blowing across the cape when the assistant lightkeeper heard cries for help. The Coast Guard in Bamfield was contacted at 11 p.m. and a lifeboat, towing an inflatable boat, headed toward Cape Beale with a crew of four.

A light was spotted where breakers were crashing on the shore and two men clinging to a partially-inflated rubber boat were picked up in the Coast Guard's inflatable. One was severely hypothermic. Two other men, the survivors told them, were also aboard the fishboat *Bruce I* when it went down. Debris from the wreck littered the seas as the lightkeeper and his assistant scanned the shores with flashlights, keeping constant radio contact with the crew aboard the lifeboat. Victoria's Search and Rescue Centre was called and informed that a voice could be heard calling for help but no one was visible and the breakers prohibited the lifeboat crew from landing on shore. The rescue centre said an American Coast Guard helicopter, with a crew of three, had been dispatched from Port Angeles, 160 kilometres away on the opposite side of Juan de Fuca Strait.

The helicopter made several passes with its searchlights and plucked a man from the rocks. But before the search could continue for the last victim the helicopter needed fuel. Arrangements were made to refuel at Tofino, where the airport normally operates only during daylight. Firepots would be ignited and as many cars as possible would illuminate the runway. While making one last pass at Cape Beale, the helicopter's engine died and it dropped 60 metres out of the sky into the stormy seas.

The lightkeeper, equipped with radio and flashlight, guided the lifeboat into shore. One man was on deck, straightening the spotlight, when an enormous wave broke over the boat, tossing it broadside down on the rocks. But she righted herself and headed back into the waves away from shore. The helicopter was spotted being thrashed about by the breakers and when the inflatable was about to be cast off from the lifeboat, the chopper's rotor suddenly appeared over the bow. The lifeboat backed off, the inflatable rushed over and everyone inside the helicopter, unharmed, scrambled aboard, abandoning the disabled aircraft to the ravage of the sea.

They were taken to the Red Cross Outpost in Bamfield and the lifeboat returned to Cape Beale. A Buffalo aircraft from Comox Armed Forces Base, on eastern Vancouver Island, illuminated the cape with flares and the search for the missing man continued. But the lifeboat encountered engine trouble and returned to Bamfield. When she was hauled out later both propellers were entangled with rope.

The Coast Guard crew returned to Cape Beale in another boat and searched until 1 o'clock in the afternoon, when they were summoned to search for two other missing fishermen. The Coast Guard crewmen had endured the gruelling ordeal at Cape Beale for 14 hours and picked up six survivors. The one they missed was never seen again.

Keeha Beach

Keeha Beach is a wild stretch of sand and driftwood bordered by impenetrable rain forests on one side and foaming surf on the other. It's only three kilometres from the head of Bamfield Inlet yet hardly anyone goes there. There's a sea cave on the western end, and water in a creek running from Kichha Lake on the east end. Keeha Beach is a good destination for a day hike, or a great spot to camp.

The Keeha Beach trail is a fork off the Cape Beale trail. To get to the start you must travel by boat, 2.5 kilometres from the government wharf in Bamfield East to the head of Bamfield Inlet. The trail to Cape Beale and Keeha Bay is marked by surveyor's tape and old floats. The sign-posted fork to Keeha Bay is about 20 minutes from the start.

It's a one-hour hike, and like the trail to Cape Beale, it's rough and soggy but reasonable for adventuresome children. There are steep hills near the end, so steep that some kind souls have tied ropes to trees on the hilltops to help hikers clamber up. If you are three years old, or are in comparable shape to a typical three-year-old, don't try this hike. Wear good boots, long pants and carry water and wet-weather clothing.

The first views of Kichha Lake appear about 40 minutes from the start of the hike. A log across a backwater off the end of the lake serves as a bridge and some considerate person has strung a rope over the bridge to act as a rail. A short distance past the bridge you can hear the waves rolling onto the beach. The steep hills are over with a few grunts and the forest opens up as the trail descends to the beach.

It's always such a dramatic feeling when you step out of the woods onto a west coast beach. Your eyes pop wide open and you wonder why the rest of the world isn't here. It's a phenomenal reward that confronts you as your environment instantly changes from the quiescent luxuriance of a rain forest to a moving panorama of sea and shore. The mud on your ankles and aches in your legs are immediately forgotten.

Sea cave at Keeha Beach

BARKLEY SOUND SALMON FISHING — CANADA'S BEST

Barkley Sound is often touted as the salmon fishing capital of Canada. It's a crossroads where thousands of big chinooks and cohoes migrate to their spawning grounds in the Stamp-Somass system, at the head of Alberni Inlet, while others move down Juan de Fuca Strait toward the Fraser River. These runs provide good fishing all year, hot fishing through summer, dynamite fishing by late summer and fall.

Much of this unparalleled angling can be attributed to the Robertson Creek Hatchery, built in 1959 to introduce pink salmon to Alberni Inlet. It was expanded over the years and is designed now to produce millions of smolts annually — 9 million chinooks, 1.5 million cohoes and 250,000 steelhead trout.

On the eastern side of Barkley Sound (fishing on the western side is covered in Chapter 2) there are paved launching ramps at Poett Nook, 15 kilometres by road north of Bamfield, and at Port Désiré, on Grappler Inlet. To find the ramp at Port Désiré, turn right at the store in Bamfield and drive about 200 metres. Some fishermen with campers set up at campgrounds near the ramps while others take tents and gear out to the Deer Group or Broken Group Islands for a few days.

By the mid-1980s fishing out of Bamfield was rapidly forming the basis of a sizable tourist industry and new motels and lodges were being built to cater to sport fishermen. Some rent boats and equipment, with or without guides. Some offer fishing packages including accommodation, guides, boats and other amenities. Others have rooms which can be rented by large groups using their own boats and equipment. Some fishing charter outfits offer camping in the Broken Group or Deer Group, where clients set up a base and spend most of their time fishing from the camp. Information on charters, boat rentals, accommodation and camping, and other facilities for fishermen is available from local tourist bureaus. Write to the addresses on p. 177. For specific, up-to-date detail on fishing, talk to someone who's been out in the last day or two: in Bamfield that could be half the town.

Although there are hundreds of islands to provide shelter for Barkley Sound boaters, the open waters around Cape Beale, in Trevor and Imperial Eagle channels, and on the outer edge of the Broken Group can be nasty. For most parts of Barkley Sound car-top boats are too small and anything under five metres could be risky. Fog is a summer hazard to all boaters. To fish the area described here you need tide tables for Tofino, a compass and two hydrographic charts — number 3671, entitled *Barkley Sound*, and number 3672, *Alberni Inlet*. Chart number 3670, entitled *Broken*

Barkley Sound fishing

Group, gives a more detailed look at the Broken Group Islands. Charts can be mail ordered by writing to the Canadian Hydrographic Service at the address on p. 177. Payment must be made in advance. A catalogue and price list are available free on request. Tide tables can be ordered from the same address.

Federal fishing licences, usually available from guides or stores which sell fishing tackle, are required when taking fin fish from all tidal waters. Licences are not needed to catch shellfish, and a few anglers like to drop crab pots in Bamfield or Grappler Inlet before heading out for the day. Oysters, mussels, clams and other bivalves also make delectable meals but check to see if a paralytic shellfish ban is in effect. Copies of fishing regulations, stipulating size and catch limits, are usually available where licences can be purchased. Check them before heading out. Fisheries officers regularly patrol Barkley Sound and Parks Canada wardens are empowered to enforce certain fishing regulations in the Broken Group. There is serious concern on Canada's west coast about declining chinook salmon stocks and spot closures are often ordered in specific areas. During the year advertisements are placed in local newspapers informing sport fishermen which areas are closed and for what periods.

Northeast Barkley Sound

The bays at the northern ends of Imperial Eagle and Trevor Channels — San Mateo, Rainy Bay, Vernon Bay and Holford Bay on Tzartus Island — offer reasonable winter chinook fishing from January to March. Smaller chinooks hang around in summer and big ones, in the 12 and 14-kilogram range, appear in early spring and stay until early fall. It's a good area to troll bait, with no flasher, at depths around 20 metres.

Farther south down Trevor Channel, tyee in the 15-kilo category arrive in June before heading up Alberni Inlet. Another run appears at Sarita at the end of the summer. Spincasters do well fishing for chums in early fall from the rocks at Sarita.

The Deer Group Islands

Much of the salmon fishing in the Deer Group centres around the waters between Kirby Point, the northwest tip of Diana Island, and the south end of Sandford Island. Big northern cohoes in the five or six-kilo range appear at the end of June and smaller cohoes, two to four kilos, show up at the end of summer. These fish can be taken near the surface with flies or small spoons and a few ounces of weight. The most exciting way to catch them is bucktailing on the surface with fly rods.

Deeper trolling is usually best to take chinooks. The largest ones come in early summer.

Cape Beale

Visitors to the Cape Beale Lighthouse frequently see sport fishermen bobbing about in the swells below the cape. It's open water and bright fishermen check the weather before heading out.

Mooching or drift fishing appear to be the preferred methods off Cape Beale when cohoes and big chinooks show in August. There's good coho fishing here in early summer, particularly offshore at Soquel Bank, about five kilometres south of the cape, and at Seabird Rocks off the mouth of Pachena Bay. But these areas are exposed to the full sweep of the Pacific Ocean. Winds and swells can combine to make a rough ride for boaters venturing offshore.

Northwest Imperial Eagle Channel

There's good year-round jack chinook fishing around Swale Rock and sizable chinooks are taken by trollers and drift fishermen in summer and fall. South of the rock, chinooks linger off the eastern ends of Reeks Island and Turner Islet and occasionally in the pass between Gibraltar and Reeks islands. In Sechart Channel trollers fish depths of 45 and 55 metres along the north side of Nettle and Prideaux islands.

Cohoes roam these waters all summer and fishermen using light gear do well in July, August and September. It's a good place for bucktailing with fly rods. Although swells roll up Imperial Eagle Channel, this is a popular spot among canoeists camped at Gibraltar Island.

The Outer Broken Group Islands

Bucktailing for cohoes is at its best the first week in July off Cree Island and Meares Bluff, on the eastern side of Effingham Island. A run of big northerns begins in the middle of June and lasts three or four weeks. Smaller cohoes in the two- to-four-kilo range appear from mid-August to mid-September. They can be taken by drift fishermen or trollers using light gear.

Anglers fishing close to the rock face at Meares Bluff take chinooks all year, particularly from spring to fall. The biggest chinooks show near Effingham and Cree Islands in June and July. Effingham Bay, on the northwest side of Effingham Island, is a protected anchorage for fishermen who sleep aboard their boats. Others fishing the outer edge of the Broken Group set up camp at Gilbert Island, one of Pacific Rim Park's designated campsites.

BAMFIELD FOR PADDLERS AND ROWERS

Anyone with a rowboat, kayak, canoe or rubber dinghy can spend a lazy day poking around the docks and waterways of Bamfield. There's more than six kilometres of sheltered water, from the head of Bamfield Inlet to the head of Grappler Inlet, with extensive mudflats, islands, islets, kelp beds and lagoons. Mink, furry brown cousins of the weasel, scurry along forested shores in search of intertidal delicacies. Families of river otters may splash between the boats and floats that line the shores of Bamfield Inlet.

Head of Bamfield Inlet

Harbor seals, curious but cautious, skulk along behind unsuspecting paddlers and chattery kingfishers dive from overhanging branches. Sea lions and, occasionally, killer whales swim down the inlet while stately bald eagles watch from snag trees overhead.

Nearly everyone lives on the waterfront in Bamfield and nearly everyone has a dock. Fishermen mend their nets and repair their vessels on the floats in front of their homes. Bamfielders climb aboard boats and run up and down the inlet as naturally as most people use their cars.

From a public wharf in Bamfield East you can paddle more than two kilometres to the head of the inlet. You'll slide through a channel between Rance and Burlo islands, past Burts Island and into a shallow lagoon where geese and other waterfowl leave webbed tracks in the mud. Abandoned, graying fishboats lie rotting along the shores, and weatherbeaten cabins, some still occupied, sit on the marsh grass below the forests.

At the other end of the inlet, around the point where the Bamfield Marine Station looks across to Bamfield West, Grappler Inlet joins Bamfield Inlet. A stretch as narrow as a west coast river leads to Port Désiré, a suburb of Bamfield, a backwoods away from the bustle of Bamfield proper. You can take your boat out here or continue past a couple of unnamed islets to the head of the inlet. Eelgrass covers the shallows and, if you're lucky and fast, you could reach over the side and snaffle up a tasty Dungeness crab.

Small boats can be rented in Bamfield or you can take a cruise on a water taxi to wherever you please. If you've got a spare couple of hours it's a great way for a family to spend an afternoon.

PADDLING THE BROKEN GROUP ISLANDS

In the centre of Barkley Sound the Broken Group Islands form an intricate network of waterways that even the most novice canoeists can paddle. Crossings between the hundred-odd islands and islets are reasonably short and some islands are so close to one another that channels dry at low tides. These enchanting islands are surrounded by the forested peaks of Vancouver Island, a picturesque backdrop almost always visible to canoeists and kayakers in the Broken Group.

Near the middle of the archipelago, where furious winter winds are barricaded by the islands on the outer edge, the narrow passages are often mirror calm, like daybreak on a trout pond. But the outer islands — Austin, Wouwer, Cree, Effingham — bear the scars of violent winter storms; windswept evergreens with branches cringing away from the open sea, barren bluffs and deep caves carved by breakers bashing at exposed shorelines.

Broken Group paddlers

Adding the Broken Group to Pacific Rim National Park in the early 1970s ensured their preservation but also increased their popularity. A journey through this fascinating maze of waterways is no longer a wilderness experience. From late spring to early fall canoeists, kayakers, power-boaters and sailors congregate in the anchorages and campsites throughout the islands. Thousands of people tour the Broken Group every year.

Unfortunately not all campers conscientiously pack out what they pack in. The influx of people has compelled Parks Canada to designate seven camping areas, most near sources of fresh water, in an effort to preserve the natural heritage of the Broken Group Islands. The campsites are located at some of the most scenic beaches, in large clearings among towering cedars and in open fields. But they can become crowded: sometimes two or three dozen tents may be pitched in one area. The only facilities are out-

121

houses. There are also cabins on Jaques and Clarke islands. Anyone can use them but they must be shared with other campers.

These campsites are the meeting grounds of the Broken Group, places where people who cross paths throughout the islands over the course of a few days finally set up camp together and swap canoeing stories around the campfire. Some become friends and end up paddling together on future expeditions.

Some solitude seekers can't resist the temptation of pitching their tents in nondesignated camping areas, away from the large groups who are legally camped. Those who do may be asked by a park warden to leave: those who refuse may have their gear seized. Overall, the islands and surrounding seas encompass more than 100 square kilometres. There's lots of room to share after canoeists and kayakers disperse from the campsites. With the exception of Indian reserves on Nettle, Keith and Effingham islands, all of the land in the Broken Group is there for anyone to explore and, depending on where you go, you can spend all day virtually alone, encountering others only when it's time to set up camp.

Many of the designated campsites were used by native Indians for at least 4,000 years before the arrival of the white man in the 1770s. The 2,000 or 3,000 Indians who inhabited the Broken Group were among an estimated 10,000 who gathered shellfish, trapped herring and anchovies and hunted whales and sea lions in the waters of Barkley Sound. In the islands they were probably divided into nine groups of 250 to 400 people and though they were generally friendly toward one another there is evidence of territorial hostilities. It appears native populations in the Broken Group were declining before the white man came but the decline reached disastrous proportions after the arrival of Europeans, mainly because of smallpox.

About 175 archeological sites were discovered during surveys of the Broken Group Islands in 1982. Paddlers who follow the paths of these industrious natives will discover their middens, fish traps, canoe runs, shellfish processing areas and defensive sites. Though the evidence suggests native Indians may have inhabited the Broken Group for 4,000 years, it's possible Barkley Sound was occupied by native groups for as long as 12,000 years. There is still a great deal of archeological work to be done in Barkley Sound and some historic sites may be excavated in years ahead. Take a look at what remains but, for the sake of the future, help preserve the past by leaving these places undisturbed.

Although most waters in the Broken Group are protected from open ocean swells and high winds, there are times when rough seas force paddlers ashore for several hours, occasionally days at a time, between June and September. Summer westerlies frequently come up in the afternoon so get up early and paddle a few hours before the breezes begin. It's wise to carry some food, water, sleeping bags and a tarp when venturing away from your campsite in case you're marooned overnight by adverse weather. People who paddle to the outer edge of the islands should beware of swells which roll in from the open sea. When they reach shallow shores they wash against the rocks then slosh out again. Keep a reasonable distance from shores when paddling in swells and avoid surge channels and sea caves. Swells are also hazardous around reefs, particularly on an ebbing tide. If you're paddling in narrow, reef-ridden channels a rock a few inches below the surface may suddenly appear in the trough between swells. If you happen to be over the rock your boat could come down on it and get holed or capsized.

Reefs are also a nuisance if you happen to hit one when clipping along at three or four knots. Every summer a few canoes, sailboats and runabouts crunch onto unseen reefs because the skippers ignored their charts, or didn't carry any at all. In 1985 Parks Canada and the Canadian Hydrographic Service cooperatively produced a new chart for the Broken Group Islands. Number 3670, entitled *Broken Group*, at a scale of 1:20,000 shows the islands in detail and provides additional information on locations of campsites, cabins and fresh water. On the back of the chart are pointers for boaters in Barkley Sound, and information on facilities, history, wildlife, hazards, suggested activities, fishing and shellfish. For an overview of Barkley Sound, which is required if you plan to paddle from Bamfield, get chart 3671 entitled *Barkley Sound*. The provincial government sells a topographic map of Barkley Sound, number 92C/14, which shows interesting land features not found on hydrographic charts. Provincial topographic maps and federal hydrographic charts can be mail ordered by writing to the addresses on p. 177. Mail orders must be prepaid and prices and chart catalogues are available free on request. With the charts you'll need a compass in case you get lost in the fog, a summer hazard which often persists for days on end in Barkley Sound.

Although tidal currents pose no problems for Broken Group paddlers, tide tables for Tofino, which can be ordered with charts, are necessary to keep an eye on tide changes. Some rocky shores are difficult to land on at low tides. Reefs, of course, are nearer to the surface at low tides. People who are accustomed to canoeing lakes may overlook tides: every summer a few canoeists return from a walk in the woods to find their boats drifting away on a flood tide. Always pull your boat high above the water's edge and tie it to something on shore. If it's full of junk and you can't be bothered to carry it up the beach for a half-hour walk, then make an anchor by tying the bowline around a boulder, leaving enough slack for the boat to float if the tide comes in. If you're paddling between late April and the end of October, when Daylight Saving Time is in effect, remember to add an hour to the times shown on the tide tables.

Tide tables are also useful for fishermen. The best times to fish are generally an hour and a half before and after tide changes. Fishing licences are required in the Broken Group Islands for all fin fish, meaning salmon, cod, halibut and other bottom fish. The islands are regularly patrolled by fisheries officers, and park wardens are empowered to enforce regulations concerning size and catch limits. There are numerous reefs and shorelines to fish for cod and salmon but paddlers should not come to the Broken Group intent on living off the land: sometimes the fish just don't bite. If you're relying on your angling skills to fill your belly you may lie awake at night listening to it growl. Licences are not needed to collect shellfish but a paralytic shellfish ban is almost always in effect in the Broken Group. It is illegal and dangerous to eat bivalves — oysters, clams, mussels and other molluscs with two hinged shells. The ban does not apply to shrimp, prawns or crabs.

During summer a park warden is stationed in a float cabin at Nettle Island in a bay due north of the campsite on Gibraltar Island. You can go there for help in an emergency but the warden is usually out on patrol during the day. Leave a note if the problem can wait: if it can't, flag down a boat with a radio. If a problem arises on a day when the *Lady Rose* is passing through, try and get to the float at Gibraltar Island for the arrival of the ship. There are usually enough people close by to help in an emergency. A first aid kit should be part of any paddler's normal camping gear.

Anyone who's been caught in a pitiless west coast downpour is well aware of the need for good quality wet-weather gear. Don't go with cheap rain suits that will split in the crotch and under the arms the moment you kneel down and take a few sweeps with a paddle. Other equipment needed in the Broken Group includes life jackets, a spare paddle, a sponge to mop up water in the stern, warm, windproof clothing and a plastic tarp or two. Matches in waterproof containers should be carried all the time. Twenty-three-litre plastic buckets with airtight lids make excellent packing containers which also provide extra buoyancy if you flip over. Sleeping bags, food, cameras, clothes, cooking utensils and other equipment can be stuffed in the buckets and lashed to thwarts and seats.

Driftwood is scarce in the Broken Group so a stove is needed for cooking. It's illegal to cut wood from the forests and fires are permitted only below the high-tide mark or in established fire circles. Fresh water, which should be boiled, may also be scarce in summer. During dry summers the water near designated campsites is barely palatable. It's best to carry a minimum of a litre of fresh water per day for each person, more if you can handle it. Dried soups which are loaded with monosodium glutamate are not recommended because they can make you terribly thirsty.

Getting There — As Paddler or Passenger

Only experienced kayakers should attempt to cross Imperial Eagle Channel from Bamfield to get to the Broken Group Islands. From the entrance to Bamfield Inlet it's a two-kilometre paddle across Trevor Channel to the Deer Group Islands, then at least another nine kilometres of open water to the Broken Group. Both Trevor and Imperial Eagle channels are exposed to swells and strong winds.

A safer route is from Toquart Bay on the northwest side of Barkley Sound. Toquart Bay is accessible by a rough dirt road from Highway 4 near Kennedy Lake. It's a logging road which could be closed during times of extreme fire hazard: check with MacMillan Bloedel forest company in Ucluelet. Drive slightly more than 85 kilometres from Port Alberni toward Long Beach and watch for a road running parallel to the highway on the opposite side from the lake. It's a bumpy 16 kilometres to Toquart Bay where you may find hundreds of campers. You can launch off the beach, paddle through the Stopper Islands and across to Lyall Point. Watch for wind around the point and, if all's well, scoot across to Hand Island, one of the designated campsites in the Broken Group.

Unloading Lady Rose *at Gibraltar Island*

The laziest way to get to the Broken Group is to load your boat and gear aboard the *Lady Rose* in Port Alberni, have a home-cooked breakfast on board and arrive in the islands in time for lunch. Boats are loaded through a hatch in the foredeck and camping gear is placed on pallets and lowered through the same hatch. It's a pleasant three-hour cruise down Alberni Inlet, through Junction Passage and across Imperial Eagle Channel to Gibraltar Island, a distance of about 60 kilometres. At Gibraltar, boats and gear are unloaded onto a float, with the help of disembarking passengers, through a door in the hold. By some secret method, the crew always manages to load and unload as many as two dozen boatloads of camping gear without mixing it up, an amazing accomplishment. The ship travels through the islands en route to Ucluelet from late spring to early fall, dropping off and picking up canoeists and kayakers several times a week. Paddlers can also board the ship at Ucluelet. You should reserve space for your boat, or make arrangements to rent a canoe or kayak through Alberni Marine Transportation Incorporated, operators of the ship, who say it's wise to try and make reservations a month in advance.

Paddlers waiting for the *Lady Rose* to take them home usually arrive a few hours before the ship or camp at Gibraltar Island on their last night in the islands. By the time the old freighter steams through the channel between Jaques and Gibraltar islands the tiny float is piled high with camping paraphernalia. There's always a lot of excited chatter about the adventures of the past week or so and the *Lady Rose* is occasionally greeted by cheering and applause. It's a farewell party and nearly everyone involved is in good spirits for the journey up Alberni Inlet. The *Lady Rose* is a highlight for paddlers who take her to the Broken Group.

Organizing the Journey

If you look at a chart of the Broken Group you'll see that the islands appear to be divided into clusters. Each cluster has at least one designated campsite which makes a good base from which to explore the entire cluster. From the campsite at Gibraltar Island, for example, you could spend a day or so touring Nettle, Prideaux, Jarvis, Jaques, Reeks, Dempster, Mullins, Onion and Wiebe islands. South of these islands, across Coaster Channel, the campsite on Gilbert Island makes a good base for travels around Effingham, Cooper, Wouwer and other islands on the outer edge of Barkley Sound. West of Gilbert there are campsites on Benson and Clarke and north of Clarke there's a campsite on Turret Island where you can set up to explore a string of islands and islets off the western end of Turret. Another cluster centred around the campsite on Willis, includes Dodd, Turtle and several

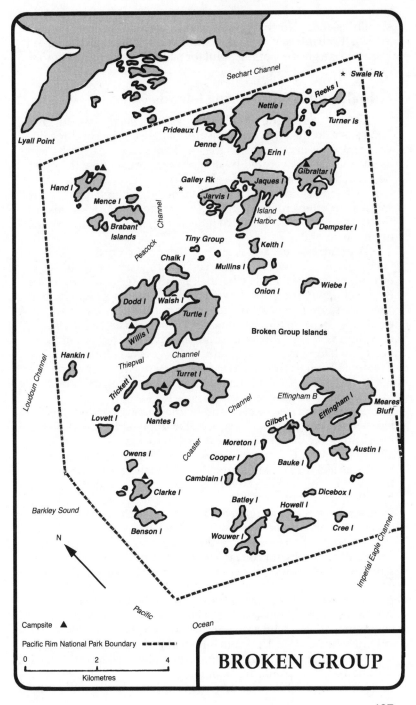

Campsite ▲

Pacific Rim National Park Boundary ▪▪▪▪▪▪▪

0   2   4

Kilometres

BROKEN GROUP

smaller islands. North of Dodd Island, across Peacock Channel, are the Brabant Islands and Hand Island, where a designated campsite is a good stopping point for paddlers coming in from To-quart Bay.

Gibraltar and Neighboring Islands

On the north side of Gibraltar Island a small, tree-covered knoll sits near the main camping area. There are two or three private campsites in clearings on the knoll but you have to grab them as soon as they're vacated by outgoing canoeists. Like the other designated campsites in the Broken Group, Gibraltar is a pretty island with shell and gravel beaches facing a sheltered harbor. The campsite is often crowded on days when the *Lady Rose* arrives but there are several places to pitch tents in big clearings in the woods or on the beaches.

A group of reefs and islets in a bay on the northeast side of Gibraltar offers some reasonable cod fishing. Farther up the western side of Imperial Eagle Channel, north of Reeks Island, Swale Rock is known as one of Barkley Sound's hot spots for chinook and coho salmon. Swells roll up the channel from the open sea but canoeists often fish the shorelines of Turner Islet and Reeks Island on calm evenings. On some summer days the foghorn at Cape Beale, 16 kilometres to the south, bellows across Imperial Eagle Channel. Though the weather may be perfectly clear along the northwest edge of the Broken Group, a soupy fog enshrouding the cape may easily be seen from Swale Rock.

The pass between Reeks and Nettle Island is dotted with islets where narrow channels are like topless tunnels. Belted kingfishers like these shallow waters and rock crabs can occasionally be picked up near the shores. Reeks Island, as the chart shows, is like three islands joined by thin land necks. Look for a tunnel near one of these land necks: you can't paddle through it but it's worth exploring. There are ancient Indian canoe runs, places where rocks were cleared to make a clean path up the beach, on Nettle Island where it faces Reeks.

Through the channel on the northwest side of Gibraltar there's good fishing for cod and small salmon. Try trolling a silver spoon with about four ounces of weight, or jig a lure, along the edge of a narrow peninsula on the south side of Jaques Island. Around the tip of the peninsula and into the bay here on Jaques Island a log cabin is nestled in the trees above the beach. It's an emergency shelter with a sleeping loft which should be shared by anyone who needs it. The cabin is built atop a large Indian midden and a few cedar trees in the surrounding forest still bear the scars of Indians cutting planks from them.

Jaques and Jarvis islands enclose the largest lagoon in the

Broken Group, a good place to watch birds and scoop up rock crabs. The channel between the islands, which leads to the lagoon from the west, may dry at extremely low tides. The lagoon, with several middens, was once a bustling site for native Indians. On the south side, where a narrow strip of land joins two large sections of Jaques Island, are three ancient fish traps. Rock walls a metre or two high were built and small fish, such as herring or anchovies, were chased to the inside of the walls on high tides. They were kept corralled, probably by children, until the tide dropped, trapping the fish between the wall and shore.

Near the mouth of the lagoon, on the west side of an islet facing Jarvis Island, is a shellfish processing area where women steamed open clam shells to take the meat. Near the processing site are three canoe runs. On the opposite side of Jarvis another canoe run and a midden are located on an islet.

There are sea caves on the southwest side of Dempster Island, interesting to visit but they should be avoided during nesting seasons. More than three dozen pelagic cormorants breed here. The craggy shores of Dempster are intriguing but good places to land are hard to find. The situation is similar across the channel west of Dempster in a group of islets around Mullins and Onion islands. Keith Island, with a nice sand and shell beach, is an Indian reserve and out of bounds to park visitors.

Hand and Brabant Islands

Hand Island is the closest designated campsite for people entering the Broken Group from Toquart Bay. It's a two-kilometre run across from Lyall Point and should be done in early morning or evening to avoid summer westerlies that funnel up Loudoun Channel. The campsite, the only one in the Broken Group without water, sits on a midden near a fish trap at the northeast end of the island. Much of the shoreline consists of jagged, barnacled boulders but the shallow bays are lined with nice shell beaches. Rock crabs scurry through the eelgrass and bottomfish linger around the reefs which surround the island. The reefs here are dangerous, so keep an eye over the bow and paddle slowly close to shore. Some people claim the water here is warm enough for summer snorkelling without a wet suit, but that depends on the thickness of your skin.

A short trail from the campsite leads to a soggy field where some rusted logging equipment on skids is hidden in the bush. There was once a trading post here but no sign of it remains. Farther along the shore on the north side an eagle's nest sits in a tree above the beach.

Hand and the Brabant Islands are separated from the rest of the Broken Group by Peacock Channel. The crossing from the northwest tip of Jarvis to the Brabants is about 1.2 kilometres. Watch for Galley Rock, an ominous unmarked reef about a third of the way across the channel. On certain tides its pointed peak sits just below the surface, often exposing itself to passing boaters between waves. It's a spooky sight, a dangerous navigational hazard which should be marked. There's good fishing for ling cod and bottomfish around Galley Rock.

The crossing from the Brabant Islands to Dodd Island is also slightly more than a kilometre. Westerly winds can be troublesome in Peacock Channel and sometimes it's necessary to travel about two kilometres to the northwest end of Dodd to avoid taking waves broadside. In calm weather you can paddle straight across to the eastern end of Dodd into a protected harbor.

Willis, Dodd and Turtle Islands

As with most islands in the Broken Group, the nicest beaches on Willis Island are on the north side. The camping beaches are sheltered by islets off the northwest end, and when the sun shines in the shallows here the water takes on a greenish tropical tinge. The main beach is a crescent-shaped stretch of sand and shells. Paths lead to large openings in the woods with views across the water.

The campsite on Willis Island may be approached from Loudoun Channel. If you decide to paddle around the western end of Dodd Island toward Willis beware of swells and winds in the channel. There are few places to pull out along the rocky western shore of Dodd so once you've decided to paddle into a westerly wind you have to stay with it until you reach Willis.

The campsite is also accessible from the east through a sheltered harbor bounded by Willis, Dodd, Turtle and Walsh islands. This area is a favorite anchorage for yachtsmen because it's protected from all summer winds. The channel between the eastern tip of Willis and the most southerly point on Dodd Island narrows to about 50 metres before opening into the harbor.

An Indian fish trap is located on the east side of a peninsula on the south end of Dodd. Farther along the Dodd Island shore is a large midden at the base of a peninsula on the island's northeast end. The beach and grassy shore here make a great spot for a picnic. Dodd Island's flat and rocky northeast shore can be reached by crossing a narrow clearing near the beach. Adjoining the clearing are the remnants of a garden planted by Salal Joe, a hermit who lived more than two decades in a float cabin at Turtle Island.

Nobody's exactly sure how Joe arrived in Barkley Sound but the story he told the author is that he immigrated to Canada after the Second World War. His real name was Joe Wilkowski and he was born in an Iranian village near the Russian border. A transient

Salal Joe

laborer in Canada, he worked his way across the country and eventually set up permanent camp at Turtle Island, probably in 1959. He never thought his dislike for seafood would be a handicap to a hermit in the Broken Group, but he attempted to solve the dilemma by planting his garden on Dodd Island.

The nickname Salal Joe was given after he began to earn a living by foraging salal from the islands and shipping it to Vancouver florists via the *Lady Rose*. During low winter tides he'd take a lamp and gather clams at night. Sacks of clams would dangle from his dock until the weather allowed him to zip across Imperial Eagle Channel to fish processors at Bamfield in *Hello Nature*, an old wooden scow with an outboard motor.

Joe wasn't a typical hermit: he had lots of friends from Bamfield and Port Alberni, many of them fishermen. He became known as the unofficial guardian of the Broken Group and earned a few dollars caretaking cabins owned by people who came only in summer. The cabin on Clarke Island was one. Among his many summer visitors was a dentist with a yacht who fixed Joe's teeth. But much of the winter for Joe and his cat Chico was long and lonely; winds would rock his cabin and rattle his dishes; heavy snows would threaten to sink his floats.

Joe was probably in his late 50s or early 60s when he died in the summer of 1980, apparently the victim of a boating accident. His scow was found impaled on the rocks near Chalk Island, the throttle on the outboard wide open. He left a will and his cabin was towed to Bamfield. The bay he inhabited on Turtle Island was officially named Joe's Bay in his honor.

With the exception of a deteriorating Indian fish trap, nothing but shells and eelgrass remain in Joe's Bay today. It's a good place to look for rock crabs. Fresh water is often available from a creek at the head of Joe's Bay.

The reefs and islets between the western end of Turtle Island and Willis make it an interesting place to paddle for people entering the protected harbor from Thiepval Channel. The harbor is also accessible from the east by paddling past the Tiny Group and the south ends of Walsh and Chalk islands.

Turret, Trickett and Lovett Islands

These three islands form an intriguing archipelago that stretches more than four kilometres from the south end of Turret to the western side of Lovett Island. Nearly two dozen islets are scattered along the southern shore of Turret Island and there are good beaches in several bays facing Coaster Channel. Beautiful sand beaches line the north side of Turret as well as the shores to the west on Trickett. Some of the channels running between the islands and islets off the western end of Turret dry at low tides.

Reefs are a hazard and winds and swells may be bothersome off the west end of Lovett.

Near the middle of Turret Island's south side is a midden and major shellfish processing area once used by native Indians. The designated campsite is also on a midden, tucked behind an islet on a point near the western end. Tent sites are above a sand beach in three or four clearings, nicely separated from one another.

The shortest distance across Thiepval Channel to Turret is about 500 metres from the southwest end of Turtle Island. There are reefs in this part of the channel, however, one of which claimed the steel-hulled minesweeper *Thiepval* in 1930. At that time the channel was unnamed and the reefs were uncharted. The ship was on winter lifesaving patrol for the federal government when she struck the reef on a falling tide. The 22 crewmen abandoned her when she started to list so seriously it appeared the ship would roll over. The crew was rescued the next day but the ship slipped into about 12 metres of water.

The *Thiepval* has since become one of Barkley Sound's most popular shipwrecks. Scuba divers have recovered several artifacts, including a cannon which was raised in 1962 and mounted for display in Ucluelet. Now that the Broken Group Islands are part of Pacific Rim National Park, no artifacts may be removed from shipwrecks in the Broken Group.

Clarke and Benson Islands

Clarke and Benson are not only the most westerly islands in the Broken Group, but probably the most beautiful. Sand and

Arriving at Clarke Island

Clarke Island camping

gravel beaches, open fields, rocky shorelines, numerous offshore islets, high cliffs and drying reefs are among the scenic features of these islands. Both have designated campsites near fresh water and Clarke Island has a cabin and float.

If you approach these islands from the campsite on Turret keep an eye out for reefs between Nantes and Owens islands. The reefs are surrounded by kelp and often pop into view between waves. This area is near the outer edge of Barkley Sound and the influence of the open Pacific — winds and swells — is particularly noticeable near the entrance to Coaster Channel.

You can pitch your tent on a beach at Clarke Island or in a clearing next to the cabin. There are sandy shores on both sides of the point where the campsite is located, facing Owens Island. An intricate series of waterways runs among islets off the northwest side. The entire western side of Clarke Island is strewn with reefs and islets.

The cabin at Clarke was obviously built to endure the wicked winter winds at the outer edge of Barkley Sound. Enormous posts and beams made from beach logs support rough cedar siding and ceilings. The floors and window frames are heavy wood and at one end of the main room is a huge fireplace made from beach stones. There's a loft above a sunken area in front of the fireplace. Counters with sinks, a pantry and wood stove are available for campers. Outside, a large wooden deck faces the beach.

A trail behind the cabin crosses the entire island. It's a pleas-ant stroll through the rain forest with side paths running down to

Benson Island

beaches. The trail passes an old concrete reservoir where you can get fresh water. Old building foundations and a wooden ramp lie rotting in the woods, gradually disappearing in the encroaching forest. Take the first fork to the right to get to a cove facing the channel between Clarke and Benson. The powerful effects of waves gnawing at the shore can be seen along one side of the cove where the bases of low cliffs have been carved away by tidal erosion.

Blow hole on Benson Island

Clarke and Benson islands were the traditional homelands of the Sheshaht Indians, one of at least nine Indian groups to inhabit the Broken Group. The Sheshaht eventually became the dominant group in the islands. The point to the east of the campsite on Clarke was what archeologists call a defensive site, a place where nearby villagers could find refuge in the event of an attack by neighboring natives.

The Benson Island campsite is at an Indian midden on the north side facing Clarke Island, sheltered from summer westerlies. You can pitch a tent on the beach or in a meadow a few metres above the high-tide line. A trail from the meadow leads to a pretty shell and gravel beach on the west side of Benson with a tall, tree-topped rock pinnacle at one end. Beyond the beach the trail forks left to a creek, or right, over some fallen logs to a beach on the outer edge of the island. The swells roll in from the open ocean here and thunder up a surge channel to a blow hole, shooting plumes of salt spray high into the air.

A sea cave on the eastern side of Benson, near the campsite, appears as a dark hole in the side of the island. The rocks around the cave look as if they'd make perfect perches for marine iguanas to bask in the afternoon sun.

The Outer Islands

Paddlers who head toward Wouwer Island from Benson Island can simply whiff the wind and follow the scent of the sea lions. You'll hear them burping and barking and splashing off the rocks as you approach. In winter more than 1,000 of these blubbery beasts, the majority of them California sea lions, line the

Wouwer Island sea lions

boulder beaches on the north side of Wouwer and south side of Batley Island. In summer the California sea lions head south but a few dozen Steller's sea lions remain on some rocks about 500 metres southwest of Wouwer. This is the only good place to get good pictures of sea lions in the Broken Group during summer. But they are on the outer edge of Barkley Sound and swells prohibit paddlers from venturing too close — you'll need a telephoto lens. These monsters are not especially interested in attacking canoes and kayaks but the big ones do weigh a tonne and should be respected.

Wouwer was a traditional fishing area for Broken Group Indians, and it's likely the ancestors of some of today's sea lions met untimely deaths at the hands of local natives. There's a major midden and canoe runs, as well as three fish traps on the jagged southeast side of the island.

Farther east, Dicebox Island was once the location of a major Indian village between two rocky knolls. Archeologists have discovered a defensive site on top of the most easterly knoll which had at least 21 homes. There is also a tunnel and sea cave on Dicebox.

Cree Island, the most southerly island in the Broken Group, was used as a lookout where Indians could keep a close watch on their neighbors and the movements of seals, sea lions, whales and other animals they hunted.

Austin Island is the site of several shipwrecks over the decades. One of the most recent was the Panamanian-registered *Vanlene*, an 8,500-ton freighter that smashed on the rocks on the east

Vanlene *before she vanished*

side of the island on March 14, 1972. She was headed to Vancouver from Japan with a crew of 38 Chinese and a cargo of 300 cars. The ship's radar, echo sounder and other navigation equipment didn't work as the ship approached the island. Breakers were spotted in the dark and the engines were put full astern. She crashed onto a reef and sent out an S.O.S., giving the location as somewhere on the Washington coast, 90 kilometres from where she really was.

Rescuers, taking bearings on the ship's transmissions, found the *Vanlene* the next day and rescued the crew. Word of the grounding drifted across Barkley Sound and scavengers swarmed the ship and stripped what they could. About half the cars were air-lifted by helicopters and for weeks new tires and car parts drifted onto the beaches of Barkley Sound. The crippled ship sat on the reef for a few years, a grim reminder to passing boaters that they were traveling near the Graveyard of the Pacific. It was an eerie sight, and people who paddled right up to it would feel shivers up their spines if the ship shifted, scraping on the rocks, while they drifted nearby. It gradually slipped farther down the reef until it vanished from sight in the late 1970s. In the mid-1980s she was sitting at depths of between 18 and 30 metres but could still slip into deeper water. The *Vanlene* has become one of the Broken Group's feature attractions for scuba divers.

East of Austin Island, more than four dozen pelagic cormorants nest on the rock ledges of Meares Bluff, Effingham Island's most easterly point. There are sea caves along the bluff and the entire eastern shoreline, right against the rocks, is a good place to troll for chinook and coho salmon throughout summer. Effingham Bay, on the opposite side of the island, is a popular anchorage for sport fishermen working the waters off Meares Bluff. This is the largest island in the Broken Group: some people refer to these islands as the Effingham Islands.

Water for the Gilbert Island campsite is found in Effingham Bay, a short distance east of the tenting area. The beach at the Gilbert Island campsite is small, bounded by rocky shores on either side. There's room for several tents in clearings above the beach where some heritage trees are located. Now protected by law, these giant cedars were stripped of their bark by Indians who wove the bark's fibres into mats, baskets, clothing and waterproof hats. On the south side of the island, near the head of a narrow cove, is a small, private spot with room for one tent. Nautical charts from the 1860s indicate there was a store on Gilbert Island, but it's definitely closed now.

If you approach Gilbert Island from Benson or Clarke, watch for westerly winds at the entrance to Coaster Channel. It's more than a kilometre to the nearest land. Winds combined with the swell can make for a nasty crossing and, though seas may appear calm when looking from Benson, you may discover halfway across that's it's not that wonderful a place to be.

The southern sides of these outer islands offer a glimpse of true west coast terrain; sea caves and wave-battered bluffs, sea lion haulouts and seabird rookeries, stunted trees and relentless ocean swells. But this is the outside edge of the Broken Group, and inexperienced paddlers should head into the swells only in ideal weather conditions or with seasoned boaters.

Gilbert Island camping

AFTER BARKLEY SOUND, WHAT NEXT?

There is no place on the southwest coast of Vancouver Island like Barkley Sound. No place where canoeists and kayakers can find sheltered waters amid a hundred islands and islets; no place where salmon fishermen can be almost guaranteed a catch; no place where you can stroll on a seaside boardwalk and see nearly every kind of boat that's ever been built.

Barkley Sound, like Long Beach, appeals to many types of outdoorsmen — hikers, divers, paddlers, sailors, anglers. But the West Coast Trail is an invitation only to those prepared to endure a week in the bush, backpacking in rugged and often wet terrain. Most agree it's a wise investment. For many, it's an adventure of a lifetime that lingers long in their memories, a tale to tell when their children and grandchildren ask what's so attractive about hiking the West Coast Trail.

CHAPTER FOUR

THE
West Coast Trail
DIFFERENT THINGS TO
DIFFERENT PEOPLE

I f you wake up on the West Coast Trail to the bellowing of a
foghorn you'll know what kind of day it is before you poke
your head out of the tent. The forests and headlands are en-
shrouded in a soft, gray mist and people along the beach appear as
hazy silhouettes. The hollow cluck of a raven may pierce the
morning air; you may even hear the snorting of a sea lion or the
whoosh of air shooting from the blowhole of a surfacing whale,
but you won't see them.

Somewhere above that vapory translucence the hot summer
sun is melting off the mist, and as you set out on the trail the seascape around you comes into focus. If you're heading toward Port
Renfrew the sun shines in your eyes as the fog lifts, revealing the
lush greens of the rain forests, the stark grays and golds of the

141

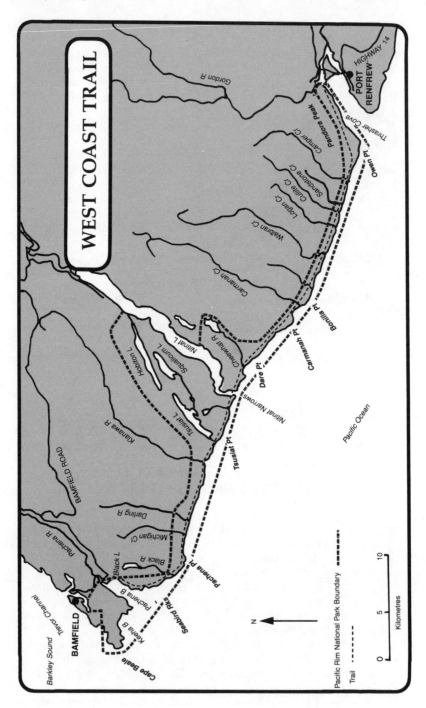

WEST COAST TRAIL

142

beaches and rocky shores. The white sails of a passing yacht, or the willowy smoke from the stack of a cargo ship may appear on the horizon, and the outline of the Olympic Peninsula comes into view across Juan de Fuca Strait. Long before noon you've reset the pace: you're well into another eventful day on the West Coast Trail.

About 5,000 hikers from around the world don backpacks and boots and set out on the West Coast Trail each year. Some hike only the first nine kilometres to Pachena Point; others continue to Tsusiat Falls or Nitinat Narrows then retrace their tracks to the start. About half of the total number of people who walk on the West Coast Trail hike it from beginning to end. It's a long, soul-stirring tramp amid some of Canada's most breathtaking scenery. It's an adventuresome challenge and those who come prepared are generously rewarded for their efforts.

People of all ages and experience hike the West Coast Trail, from elementary school kids to seasoned 70-year-old footsloggers. Some arrive decked out in the latest hiking attire, packing the best of the newest gear. Others wear soft-soled sneakers and carry old, frameless packs that bounce about on their backs with every toilsome step. Most come with reasonably good equipment, well-worn boots and carefully-planned itineraries.

The West Coast Trail is no cakewalk, it's not a place to try and lose weight or learn the basics of coastal camping. There are risks involved: some hikers have fallen from cliffs or been swept away to their deaths in surge channels. Some have broken legs and other bones. A good starting age is 12 or 13 and people who take younger children should be aware of their limitations and remember who is responsible for their safety.

But for experienced backpackers in good physical shape the West Coast Trail is among Canada's finest hikes: 72 kilometres of forest and shore along the infamous Graveyard of the Pacific. Rusted boilers and anchors, relics from tragedies of the past, bedeck the beaches where some of the ships went down. The blimpish bodies of seals and sea lions cover a few select rocks where they lie above the sea, oblivious to the waves sloshing against the shore. Through binoculars you can watch whales and porpoises sharing the seas with fishboats, freighters, yachts and ocean liners. Loons, mergansers, gulls and a variety of waterfowl swim the shores along the trail, and ravens, bald eagles, Steller's jays and other birds inhabit the forests.

The rain forests here are as impressive as the beaches: Douglas-fir, western redcedar, hemlock and sitka spruce tower above a luxuriant understory of salal and ferns, huckleberry, blueberry, blackberry, salmonberry and other moisture-loving plants.

The West Coast Trail, however, is not only a feast of rugged, wild scenery: it is, after all, a long walk on a beach, somewhere to rearrange perspectives, to become engrossed in thought without the hindrances of everyday life at home. You may walk for hours next to your best friend and never share a word, but in all likelihood you'll share similar feelings. The West Coast Trail is different things to different people, but invariably, it's more than just a walk on a wooded coast.

Starting near Pachena Bay

TO THE WEST COAST TRAIL BY LAND, SEA OR AIR

Both ends of the West Coast Trail are accessible by road. Port Renfrew, at the southeast end, can be reached via Highway 14, which begins at Colwood on the outskirts of Victoria. With the exception of a short gravel stretch, it's a 95-kilometre paved road to Port Renfrew. There is no public transportation to Port Renfrew.

The other end of the West Coast Trail can be reached by gravel logging roads from Port Alberni and Youbou, a village on the north side of Cowichan Lake. These two roads meet near Franklin River logging camp where a single road continues as far as Bamfield. Total distance from Port Alberni to the start of the West Coast Trail at Pachena Bay is 99 kilometres. From Youbou it's 105 kilometres. Youbou can be reached by taking the Lake Cowichan turnoff from Highway 1, about three kilometres north of the city of Duncan. Both logging roads are maintained according to use by forest companies which keep them open. They are open to the public year-round and, although often dotted with potholes and bumps, are passable for ordinary cars. They can be used at any time of day or week but logging trucks always have the right-of-way. The road between Port Alberni and Bamfield is unrestricted but restrictions are occasionally imposed on the road from Youbou: it could be shut down during periods of extreme fire hazard.

Many hikers leaving or beginning from Bamfield, five kilometres from the start of the trail at Pachena Bay, use the *Lady Rose*, a 31-metre cargo and passenger ship which makes several trips a week between Port Alberni and Bamfield. Island Coach Lines runs buses to major Vancouver Island centres from Port Alberni.

Pacific Rim Airlines, based in Port Alberni, runs scheduled flights to Bamfield. Charters can be arranged to be picked up or dropped off in Bamfield, Port Renfrew or Nitinat. The airline will also fly to Vancouver, Nanaimo, Victoria, Sooke and other destinations. To make arrangements call or write to the address on p. 177.

INFORMATION — HELPFUL ADVICE FOR NEWCOMERS

The best information on the West Coast Trail and surrounding areas is available from Parks Canada. Pacific Rim National Park has an information outlet in an A-framed cabin at the trail head on Pachena Bay. Another Parks Canada information centre is located in Port Renfrew, next to the recreation complex two kilometres from the trail head. The Pacific Rim Park information outlets are open during normal office hours, seven days a week from mid-May to the end of September. Parks Canada's information centre at Long Beach can also provide detail on the West Coast Trail and any other part of Pacific Rim National Park. It can be requested by phone or by writing to the address on p. 177.

Information on facilities for travellers is available from tourist information outlets in the Pacific Rim area. There is a tourist information centre in Bamfield.

ACCOMMODATION, CAMPING AND SERVICES

At the Bamfield end of the West Coast Trail there are several types of accommodation including motels, lodges, cabins and campgrounds which are described in detail in Chapter 3. Parks Canada allows campers coming and going on the trail to stay up to three nights on the beach at Pachena Bay, where there's an information centre and parking lot. It's mainly an overnight spot offered as a convenience for hikers. Long stays are discouraged.

The Ohiaht Indian band operates a campground, store, coffee shop and gas station on the Anacla Reserve, adjoining Parks Canada's property at the northern head of the trail.

A host of services is available in Bamfield, five kilometres from the start of the trail, including accommodation, general stores, a post office, outpost hospital, cafes and restaurants. There's no bank or liquor store. Showers may be available: check at local hotels or Bamfield's tourist information centre. Detail on Bamfield's services is provided in Chapter 3.

Services are not as plentiful at the southeastern trail head in Port Renfrew. There is a limited number of hotels. Local Indians allow camping on the beach near the Gordon River, where the trail begins. A forest company has a nice campground on Fairy Lake, five kilometres east of the beginning of the trail. Other amenities in Port Renfrew include a post office, a general store with a liquor outlet and a service station.

EQUIPMENT, FOOD AND CLOTHING

Once you set out on the West Coast Trail you're on your own. It's 72 kilometres to the next store and if you forget something you'll have to live without it. Careful preparation of equipment and daily planning of meals is imperative. Although meals may be supplemented by fish, hikers should not tackle the trail with the idea of living off the land. Take enough food to last two days longer than the hike and save any leftovers for the next trip if you're lucky enough to eat fresh fish every day. For people unfamiliar with coastal hiking there are a few things to remember. Expect it to rain, possibly pour. The annual rainfall at Bamfield averages 2,854 millimetres: it's one of the rainiest places in the world. Good quality wet-weather clothing, with a hat, is essential. Light rain gear used by joggers and bicyclists is usable if it's coated with a waterproofing material. There's a substantial difference between "water-resistant" and "waterproof" and on the west coast equipment should be waterproof. Tents with waterproof flies or plastic tarps are needed to keep off rain and heavy dew. Anything that can't fit in a tent at night should be covered with a tarp. A good, polyweave tarp also makes a reasonable shelter to dry clothing around a fire in the rain. Backpacks should be sprayed with a waterproofing material and boots should be coated with silicone or something similar before leaving. Everything inside a pack should be packed in plastic bags and a few extra bags may be handy for garbage and to replace ones that tear. Down sleeping bags are light, but heavier synthetic-filled bags are better in damp climes and retain their insulative qualities when wet.

Blue jeans may be durable but they suck up water like a sponge. Wool pants are more water resistant and maintain their warmth when damp. Sweat suits are comfortable for walking and are easy to slip off and on for changes in the weather. A sweater is needed after sunset and a windbreaker will keep out chilly ocean breezes. A good combination is a sweatshirt and rain jacket.

Driftwood is the only source of fuel for fires and a small hatchet may be handy. Matches in waterproof containers should be packed. Some hikers carry fire-starter cubes but a fire can always be started with a handful of dry cedar shavings and patience. Pack a good knife and sharpen it before you leave home. A backpacking stove should be carried to cook meals.

Light boots, well broken in, are among the most important items on the West Coast Trail. Don't buy a new pair of hiking boots and set off on the trail without putting a few miles on them beforehand. Uninitiated or poor-fitting boots can cause painful blisters and torn toenails, more often than not, on the first day of the hike.

At least 15 metres of rope for every two people should be carried to use as safety lines when crossing hazardous surge channels. It's also handy for stringing wet clothes around a fire and hoisting food out of reach of pesky rodents. Other materials to pack include a needle and thread, flashlight and spare batteries, bug repellent, first-aid kit, binoculars, string, toilet paper, mess kit, tooth brush and anything else you're accustomed to carrying on long hikes.

The British Columbia government, in cooperation with Parks Canada, has published a special West Coast Trail topographic map at a scale of 1:50,000. It shows the trail in detail and provides valuable information on beach accesses, campsites, stream crossings, beach walking and points of interest. It's printed on waterproof paper and can be mail ordered by writing to the address on p. 177. A compass is unnecessary but, when used with the map, adds interest to the hike. The map also suggests the safest places for beach hiking and details what tides are needed. Tide tables for Tofino, which can be copied for the period you'll be on the trail, are required, along with a watch, to determine whether it's safe to hike beaches. If you're hiking between late April and late October, when Daylight Saving Time is in effect, remember to add an hour to the times shown on the tables. The topographic map, tide tables and this book provide all the information needed for a safe and successful hike on the West Coast Trail.

HIKING TOGETHER — EIGHT IS ENOUGH

There's little more annoying than setting up camp on a pretty beach and being descended upon by an unmanageable, unruly group of neophyte hikers. The West Coast Trail is a wilderness adventure and though it must be shared with strangers, no one should be subjected to the disturbance of large, noisy groups. The trail has become popular among school groups and some leaders have been known to take as many as 60 youngsters out at once in May and June.

In fairness to other hikers, Parks Canada suggests a maximum of eight to a group. People congregate at the most commonly used camping areas. In most places there is generally room for between 10 and 20 tents, which probably means between 20 and 40 people. If a camping area is filled to capacity and a ridiculously large group suddenly appears, everyone at the campsite suffers. Overcrowding causes garbage and sanitation problems and destroys the wilderness experience.

While teenaged students should be encouraged to hike the West Coast Trail, a part of the lesson should include wilderness ethics. Large groups should be split into manageable sizes of eight or fewer and each group should camp at least a kilometre apart. By registering at the trail head Parks Canada personnel can keep tabs on the number of large groups on the trail and help you time the

148

Hiking in small groups

start of your hike to avoid overcrowding the campsites, making the journey more pleasant for everyone on the trail.

Leaders can write to Parks Canada for information on group sizes and trail conditions and to inform parks people of their plans. If others are planning to hike the trail at the same time, Parks Canada can inform them to expect other groups to be on the trail.

SAFETY AND EMERGENCIES

All parties setting out on the West Coast Trail should be properly-equipped, self-contained units without need to rely on anyone else for help. Tell a friend or relative of your plans and call them when you're out of the bush. Hikers should also register at the information centres at Port Renfrew and Pachena Bay.

First-aid kits should be water tight and contain various sized band-aids, gauze and adhesive tape, elastic bandages for sprains, moleskin and a mild antiseptic cream for blisters, a needle for slivers, aspirin, burn ointment, suntan lotion, antihistamine and any necessary prescription drugs.

Water bottles and at least two days' extra food should be carried. Water, which should be boiled, is available at several spots on the trail but there could be long stretches between good water sources, particularly during a dry summer. Matches in waterproof containers should also be carried.

On Vancouver Island, west means wet: the importance of good wet-weather clothing can't be overemphasized. Don't try and get away with cheap rain suits that split along the seams and rip at the elbows and knees. All materials inside backpacks should be packed in plastic bags or containers, especially sleeping bags and spare clothing.

Staying dry prevents hypothermia, a miserable disorder that happens as often in summer as in winter. Some hikers believe if it's raining it's best to wear only shorts and t-shirt, relying on summer temperatures to keep them warm until they can dry their clothes around an evening campfire. If it's raining, however, the sun won't be shining and it may be difficult, if not impossible, to dry wet clothes. The best defence against hypothermia is to prevent getting wet in the first place. Information on the causes of hypothermia, and how to deal with it, is provided in Chapter 1.

If a serious mishap occurs on the West Coast Trail there are usually enough people around to help. Lightkeepers at Carmanah and Pachena points can radio for help. Park wardens regularly patrol the trail and can take out an injured person by boat. Seriously injured hikers can be lifted out by helicopter, if the weather is safe for flying. There's a Red Cross Outpost hospital at Bamfield and a general hospital in Port Alberni.

CROSSING STREAMS AND WALKING BEACHES

Parks Canada has upgraded and maintained the West Coast Trail in recent years, eliminating or minimizing many of the natural hazards that previously plagued hikers. They have been careful, however, not to take the challenge out of the hike and although new bridges may span the streams, and boardwalks may cover the bogs, the hike nonetheless poses some dangers.

Ferry services at Gordon River and Nitinat Narrows are offered only from mid-May to the end of September. In other words, the southeastern 42 kilometres of the trail are virtually closed from the beginning of October to the middle of May, unless you make your own boating arrangements. Ferry operators at both crossings usually keep an eye out for hikers in need of their services. They run during the day and fares are charged. Various signals have been used to attract attention when in need of a ride from Thrasher Cove to Port Renfrew.

The first ride on a cable car across a river can be spooky. If you're apprehensive about being precariously suspended high over a rushing river, well, tough luck, you either do it or walk all the way home. A maximum of two people at a time should use a

Crossing the Klanawa River

cable car. The best method is to relax in the car while a partner pulls the cables. Any malfunctions should be reported to a park warden.

If water levels are low enough streams can be waded, using a staff for balance, keeping it on the downstream side. A few foolish hikers don't bother to take off their pants and end up shivering along the trail for the rest of the day. A single pair of sneakers can be shared among hikers for crossing streams: just throw them back across the stream when you've crossed and the next hiker can wear them. You're not likely to wade any streams that are too wide.

151

Beach hiking is something that comes with practice. On dry, sandstone surfaces at low tides it's like walking on a city sidewalk. But many rocky shores are slippery and rough and footsteps should be carefully placed to avoid falling. On sandy beaches the difficulty is sinking with each step, a problem which can become exhausting. The hardest surfaces are usually along the tide-line, marked by driftwood and weed, or right against the edge of the water.

A surge channel is a narrow gully where the force of waves rushing in and out is amplified as the water squeezes into the channel. Powerful waves gush into the surge channel, dashing anything that floats against the rocks, then sweep back out, sucking debris out to sea. People have drowned in surge channels on the West Coast Trail. About 15 metres of rope for every two hikers should be carried to use as safety lines to prevent falls when crossing surge channels. If a surge channel appears slightly over-challenging, forget it and return to the trail.

The beaches along the West Coast Trail are the main routes for hikers. They are usable, however, only under certain tidal conditions.

CAMPING COURTESY— VANISHING WITHOUT A TRACE

There's a certain satisfaction in looking back as you start another day on the West Coast Trail and seeing no trace of the previous night's campsite. You may have spent the evening huddled around a campfire, rearranging gear and planning the next day, but when you've gone the site appears as though no one had ever been there. It's a courtesy to those who follow, and a small reward for yourself.

The most popular campsites on the West Coast Trail are Thrasher Cove, Camper Bay, Walbran Creek, the Cheewhat River, Tsusiat Falls, the Klanawa River, Darling River and Michigan Creek. In spite of their popularity it's possible to set up a reasonably private campsite. Tents should be pitched and human wastes should be buried at least 30 metres from fresh water sources and at least 30 centimetres deep. Unfortunately, not all campers are discreet about where they deposit human wastes and in some areas it's like walking in a mine field. Toilet paper can be burned.

A good fire is large enough to dry clothing, cook meals and burn combustible garbage but doesn't need to illuminate half the beach. Plastic and aluminum foil won't burn and should be taken home, along with any other litter you may find, if you've got room for it. Use only driftwood, let it burn right down and douse the coals thoroughly before leaving. Ashes should be buried deep enough so that the next group of hikers won't tread in dirty black charcoal as they set up camp. The cleanest and most reliable heat source for cooking is a small camp stove.

West Coast Trail camping

Although drinking water is usually plentiful on the West Coast Trail it should be boiled. Clothing, dishes and tired bodies should be washed at least 30 metres from fresh water sources. Some items, including people, can be washed without soap, but if soap is necessary use a biodegradable variety. Dishes can also be washed in the ocean, using sand and gravel to scour utensils, pans and plates. Campers who leave uncleaned dishes until morning may awaken to the scritch-scratching of mice foraging among pots and pans. Mice, mink, martens and racoons are frequent nocturnal visitors to West Coast Trail campsites: if possible, hang food out of reach.

153

Sleeping under the stars on the west coast is an unforgettable experience if you can tolerate sand fleas bouncing off your sleeping bag. Besides a ground sheet, a tarp should be used to cover your bag and keep off heavy dew. Morning moisture may soak anything around a campsite which is left uncovered. Cheap, plastic tarps have a habit of tearing and getting discarded in conspicuous places along the West Coast Trail: use a good polyweave tarp.

A tidy, well-organized campsite is easy on the eye and simple to dismantle quickly for an early start the next day.

WEST COAST TRAIL FISHING — REFRESHINGLY FRESH

Fishing along the West Coast Trail can provide a welcome change from freeze-dried goop and cheese sandwiches. A small backpacking rod with a spinning reel and some light lures doesn't take much room. Half a dozen hooks and a few metres of nylon line is sufficient equipment to hoist a fish from a sheltered cove or gully.

Federal licences are needed to fish in saltwater and provincial fishing licences are required for streams and lakes. Regulations are usually available where you can buy licences and tackle. Licences aren't required to take shellfish such as oysters, clams or mussels but a ban could be in effect due to paralytic shellfish poisoning. Ask at the information centres at either end of the trail.

Cod and bottomfish provide the best prospects for summer fishermen who cast off rocky shores and headlands into deep water. Greenling, black bass and other rockfish linger among kelp beds near shore. They're nocturnal fish and are taken most often at dusk or after dark when they come close to the surface. Find an opening in the kelp and cast into it. Stand above the weed line to avoid slipping, especially if you're fishing in the dark.

Some of these fish, particularly greenling, swim into weed-filled gullies and coves. You can break open a mussel or clam for bait and dangle a hook in a metre or so of water to catch them. They're not large fish but a couple of fillets from one make a nice meal for two.

Evening fishing for coho salmon near the mouths of rivers isn't bad in August, September and October. Coho fishing off the mouth of the Cheewhat River after a heavy October rain can be excellent. The Cheewhat and other streams with shallow estuaries provide reasonable sea-run cutthroat fishing in early fall. Use small spinners or flies. The Klanawa River is known for fair coho runs in fall, and summer steelhead, but you'll have to go upstream from the mouth for steelhead.

WINTER HIKING — SUNSHINE AND FROST

Some of the nicest days of the year on the West Coast Trail happen in the dead of winter. With the mild temperatures of the southwest coast there are periods in winter when hikers can walk part of the day in t-shirts. But when the sun goes down, or a breeze blows in from the open ocean, the cold bites through your skin right to your bones.

There are no ferry services at Gordon River or Nitinat Narrows during winter so hikers who want to walk the entire trail must make their own crossing arrangements. The section from Nitinat to Pachena Bay can be hiked at any time of year and you may have the trail to yourself.

Violent winter storms, with seas lashing the shores and howling winds shaking the tops of the trees, are a spectacular sight for warmly-dressed hikers. Sheltered campsites can be found even in storms but winter hikers should always check weather before leaving home and be prepared for unexpected changes. Snow is a rarity on the trail but frost is a hazard on bridges and boardwalks. Exposed roots and rocks are slippery and mud is irritating on wet winter days.

Winter camping, particularly on Vancouver Island's wet west coast, is a specialized pastime. Few, if any, other people are in the area to help in an emergency. But hikers prepared to deal with potential hazards can enjoy an entirely different experience from those who walk the West Coast Trail in summer.

OFF THE BEATEN TRACK

There are two interesting side trips off the West Coast Trail which involve the Nitinat Lakes. Hikers can meet friends who have canoed to Nitinat Narrows or Little Tsusiat Lake and swap car keys. The canoeists then set out on the trail while the hikers become canoeists. Everyone meets later at some prearranged destination.

The meeting point closest to Nitinat Narrows is Brown Cove, reached by a rough 2.4-kilometre trail from Clo-oose. The trail passes Clo-oose Lake, a good spot to try catching some cutthroat trout. From Brown Cove it's a 19-kilometre paddle up the eastern shore of Nitinat Lake to a campsite near the mouth of the Nitinat River.

Canoeists can also make it as far as Little Tsusiat Lake, which is accessible by a path off the West Coast Trail above Tsusiat Falls. The return trip by canoe involves at least one, possibly two, horrible portages. Once in Nitinat Lake, canoeists can either paddle to the campsite near the mouth of the Nitinat River or pull out at Knob Point on the northwest end of the lake.

THE WEST COAST TRAIL — A LIFELINE FOR SHIPWRECK VICTIMS

More than 50 ships have met their doom along the stretch of perilous coast between Pachena Bay and Port Renfrew. After 1890, when a telegraph line between Victoria and Cape Beale was strung from tree to tree, shipwrecked sailors could find shelter in linemen's cabins, spaced along a primitive path used to maintain the telegraph line. But a good route to civilization didn't exist, and it wasn't until one of the worst marine disasters on the southwest coast of Vancouver Island occurred that a decision to construct and maintain a trail through the jungle-like bush was made.

The *Valencia*, an American steamer of nearly 1,600 tons was en route from San Francisco to Victoria and Seattle with a total of 164 crew and passengers aboard. In poor visibility the captain overshot the entrance to Juan de Fuca Strait by more than 60 kilometres. Just after midnight on Jan. 22, 1906, the ship ran aground seven kilometres east of Pachena Point. The captain ordered the engines reversed and the *Valencia* slipped off the rock. But she was taking water through a hole in the bow at an alarming rate and the captain decided to put her back on the rocks to avoid sinking. She grounded about 50 metres from shore.

Pandemonium set in and panicking passengers began taking to lifeboats, only to be capsized and lost in the pounding surf. Attempts to fire lifelines ashore with harpoons failed. A few who'd abandoned ship made it to shore and a lineman's cabin with a telephone was found. Word was sent to Victoria, 15 hours after the ship went aground. Meanwhile, another lifeboat party made it to Pachena Bay and its crew hiked to Cape Beale Lighthouse.

Rescuers arrived by ship and shore a day and a half after the grounding but they were unable to approach the ship to rescue survivors. Heavy seas were crashing over the decks and survivors were clinging to the rigging. As rescuers looked on helplessly an enormous wave broke above the ship, turning her over, tossing her ill-fated passengers into the sea.

By the time the terrifying ordeal had ended, only 38 of the 164 people aboard were alive. Fifty-nine bodies were recovered and the others were declared missing and presumed drowned. The summer after the tragedy, Indians exploring a cave near the wreck found a lifeboat from the *Valencia* with eight skeletons aboard.

The catastrophe prompted the construction of a good trail to aid shipwreck victims in finding a route out of the bush and to allow rescuers to get to wreck sites quickly. The building of a road 4 metres wide from Bamfield to what later became known as Valencia cliffs was started in 1907, the same year Pachena Point Lighthouse was established. A trail 1.5 metres wide was built to Carmanah Point and beyond Carmanah the rough telegraph route was improved.

It become known as the Lifesaving Trail or the Shipwrecked Mariner's Trail and on Dec. 20, 1911 was officially designated a public highway. But with improved navigational aids the need for the trail diminished, along with trail maintenance, over the years. It was virtually forgotten until the 1960s when recreationists began a campaign to rescue the trail from encroaching rain forests. Plans to create a new national park on the southwest coast of Vancouver Island were in the works and interested groups pushed to have the trail included.

Thanks to their untiring efforts, people today, and for generations to come, can hike this historic trail. Parks Canada undertook a trail reconstruction program in 1973, which was substantially completed by 1980. The trail from Pachena Bay to Carmanah was rebuilt and beyond Carmanah it was upgraded.

There is a viewpoint on the West Coast Trail overlooking the site of the *Valencia* grounding but no wreckage remains visible.

THE WEST COAST TRAIL FROM PORT RENFREW TO PACHENA BAY

It doesn't much matter at which end you begin the 72-kilometre hike along the West Coast Trail: the scenery's the same either way. The going's rougher from Carmanah to Port Renfrew and some hikers prefer to get it over with, leaving the less rugged sections near Pachena as a treat at the end of the walk. Many of these southeast-end starters also have trouble mustering enthusiasm for the climb up the southwest slopes of Pandora Peak, between Port Renfrew and Thrasher Cove, so they avoid it by catching a boat ride directly to Thrasher Cove.

Other hikers believe in starting off, packs fully loaded, on the easier northwest end, giving themselves a few days to set the pace and lighten the loads in their backpacks.

If you're relying on public transportation to get back to civilization it would be best to find a way to Port Renfrew and hike toward Pachena Bay. From there you can walk or hitch a ride to Bamfield, take the *Lady Rose* to Port Alberni and a bus to any major Vancouver Island centre or ferry terminal. If the hike is part of a longer outdoors vacation, there is also a greater variety of ac-

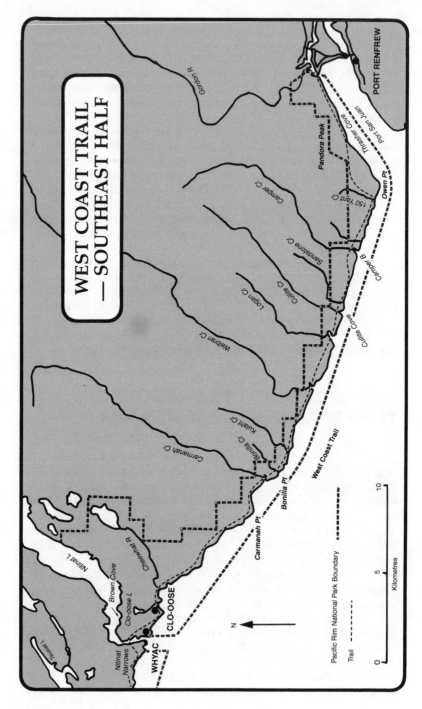

WEST COAST TRAIL
—SOUTHEAST HALF

tivities and facilities available in Bamfield than in Port Renfrew, particularly for people without cars. You could take other hikes to Cape Beale, Tapaltos Bay or Keeha Bay; rent canoes or kayaks and have a local charter boat owner drop you in the Broken Group Islands or Deer Group Islands for a few days. A day or two of salmon fishing is a pleasant way to wrap up a week-long hike; you could rent a boat or go out with a guide in Barkley Sound. Boats can also be chartered for a ride across Barkley Sound to Ucluelet where you can catch a taxi or bus to Long Beach.

Chapter 3, which covers Barkley Sound, has several suggestions for outdoors holidays which may be of interest to people coming off the West Coast Trail with a few days to spare.

Beach walking

Gordon River to Camper Bay

Distance: 11.5 kilometres

Anyone who climbs along the southwest slopes of Pandora Peak can understand why many hikers take a boat directly to Thrasher Cove and begin the hike there. The West Coast Trail starts at a fishing boundary marker near the mouth of the Gordon River. It's uphill from here as the trail climbs to 180 metres above sea level, the highest point on the trail. This beginning section can

Derelict equipment

be muddy and slippery where several small creeks run down the cliffs toward Port San Juan. A short distance before the summit, a little better than halfway to Thrasher Cove, a derelict donkey engine sits near the trail.

Thrasher Cove is reached by a side trail which begins 4.8 kilometres from the Gordon River. It's about a half-hour walk to the cove from the West Coast Trail and ladders lead down to the beach, a good campsite. From here you can return to the trail or, if tides are below 2.4 metres, hike the shoreline. From the Thrasher Cove trail junction the West Coast Trail veers off into the woods, moving more than a kilometre inland at some points. There are good views across the sea from openings in the forest along the trail. It returns to the seashore about a kilometre beyond Owen Point.

If tides are low enough you can walk nearly six kilometres along the beach to an access path which returns to the main trail before Camper Bay. The sandstone immediately beyond Owen Point is like the surface of the moon: holes of varying width and depth are teeming with marine life. The engine block and shaft from the fishboat *Apache Hunter*, which was wrecked near 150 Yard Creek in 1984, sits on the beach a kilometre past Owen Point. Slightly more than a kilometre beyond the creek is a dangerous surge channel which can be crossed at low tides when traveling toward Camper Bay. The shelf along this stretch of beach can be hiked only at low tides.

A path connects the beach to the main trail which runs through a blow-down area, where windblown trees lie scattered across the forest floor, before heading down toward Camper Bay. Ladders lead to Camper Creek and a cable car crosses Camper Bay to a good campsite.

Camper Bay to Walbran Creek

Distance: 8.8 kilometres

If the tide is below 1.7 metres you can walk on the beach from Camper Bay to Sandstone Creek. There's a hazardous surge channel near the mouth of the creek but it's passable at low tides. There is, however, an impassable headland beyond Sandstone Creek. A path up the creek leads to the main trail and a bridge. A cable car crosses Cullite Creek and there's good camping at Cullite Cove.

A boardwalk covers a swampy area between Cullite and Logan creeks. There's another good campsite near the mouth of Logan Creek, which can be crossed by bridge after a steep descent. You can return to the beach at Logan Creek and walk all the way to Walbran Creek. The main obstacle is a surge channel near a waterfall just over a kilometre from Logan Creek. A tide below

1.7 metres is needed to pass the channel and the rocks around it are slippery. To walk the rest of the way to Walbran Creek, tides must be down to 2.1 metres or lower. A cable car crosses Walbran Creek where there's good swimming and camping.

Walbran Creek to Carmanah Point

Distance: 9.3 kilometres

A short distance west of Walbran Creek you can step onto a long, sandy beach and walk almost all the way to Carmanah Point. A tide of 3 metres or lower is needed to walk the first 2 kilometres to Vancouver Point. A path crosses the point if tides are too high to walk around it. The West Coast Trail also runs through the woods from Walbran Creek to a spot just beyond Vancouver Point, where it leads to the beach. From here it's beach walking for about l.5 kilometres then the trail moves back up from the beach. If the tide is below 3.6 metres you can continue on the beach to Bonilla Point where a bridge crosses Bonilla Creek.

You can pitch a tent here and comb the shores for artifacts from ill-fated ships which met untimely ends around Bonilla Point. Relics from the wrecks must be left where you find them. There are a few remains from the *Lizzy Marshall*, a three-masted barque which was thrown ashore by a gale in February, 1884. Her hull broke in two and all but one of her 13 crewmen survived. There are also remnants from the four-masted schooner *Puritan* which became stranded in bad weather in November, 1896. A lone Indian on the shore managed to secure a line from the stern of the ship to the shore and rescue the 10 crewmen. The ship broke apart the next day and the Indian was later rewarded for his heroic efforts. The remains of other vessels which met with disaster at Bonilla Point in more recent years are still visible on the beaches at low tides.

There's more beach walking beyond Bonilla Point to Carmanah Point. A cable car crosses Carmanah Creek, where there's a good campsite. The hike returns to the forest just before Carmanah Point Lighthouse and goes around behind the lighthouse grounds. A short distance past the lighthouse, built in 1890, about 100 Steller's sea lions haul out on the rocks in both summer and winter.

Carmanah Point to Nitinat Narrows

Distance: 12.4 kilometres

The West Coast Trail from Carmanah Point Lighthouse goes through the woods for about 2.5 kilometres before returning to the beach at a place known as "the Cribs" where there's a natural breakwater. It's a good place to camp but beware of thousands of seagulls in summer.

Harbor seals

Beyond the headland northwest of the bay you can take the trail or walk the beach all the way to Dare Point at low tides, but there's a tough surge channel a little better than halfway to the point. A tide of 2.7 metres or lower is needed to pass it. There's a rusted old boiler on the beach here, a relic from the steel steam schooner *Santa Rita* which ran aground in a gale in February, 1923. Her 30 crewmen managed to get ashore.

If you take the trail to Dare Point you'll walk above the cliffs before climbing down a long staircase and boardwalk to the beach. You can hike the trail or beach to the Cheewhat River bridge and campsite. As you cross the bridge look for old hull timbers from the wreck of the *Raita*, which drifted ashore in January, 1925.

Stick to the trail beyond the Cheewhat River to Clo-oose where old cabins, gardens and gravestones can be seen in the bush above the shore. There's a good viewpoint near Clo-oose and an anchor on the rocks below. The anchor is all that remains of the *Skagit*, a three-masted barquentine that was tossed ashore by stormy seas in October, 1906. The captain and cook perished but eight crewmen were rescued. Look for petroglyphs on the beach here. If you think you hear a cow mooing lethargically from somewhere off Clo-oose, you're hearing a whistle buoy. It's an aid to navigation activated by waves which compress air in the buoy, blowing the horn.

Stay on the trail to Whyac, where there's an Indian village near Nitinat Narrows. Local summer residents operate a ferry service across Nitinat Narrows from mid-May to the end of September. For a small fee someone will take you either direction across the narrows in most tides and weather.

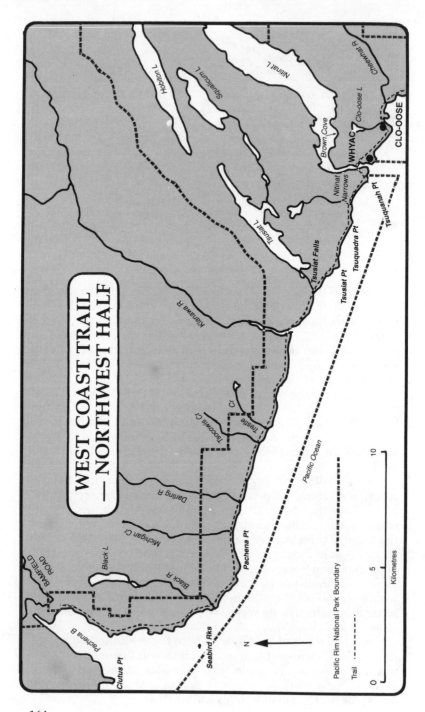

WEST COAST TRAIL
— NORTHWEST HALF

Pacific Rim National Park Boundary

Trail

Kilometres

0   5   10

N

Pacific Ocean

Seabird Rks

Clutus Pt

Pachena B

BAMFIELD ROAD

Black L

Black R

Michigan Cr

Darling R

Pachena Pt

Tsocowis Cr

Trestle Cr

Klanawa R

Tsuquanah Pt

Tsuquadra Pt

Tsusiat Pt

Tsusiat Falls

Tsusiat L

Nitinat Narrows

WHYAC

Brown Cove

Clo-oose L

CLO-OOSE

Cheewhat R

Nitinat L

Squalicum L

Hobiton L

Nitinat Narrows to Klanawa River

Distance: 9.2 kilometres

About 1.3 kilometres west of Nitinat Narrows the West Coast Trail returns to the beach. You can stay on the trail or walk the beach almost all the way to Tsusiat Falls. There are sea caves and rock galleries at Tsuquadra Point. A short detour must be made over the top of the point and you can return to the beach and head toward Tsusiat. You may find an anchor and other fittings on the beach about a kilometre east of Tsusiat Point. They're from the three-masted schooner *Vesta* which was lost on the beach in November, 1897. She was thrown so high on the shore that her masts ended up in the bush.

There are more sea caves and the well known "Hole in the Wall," a tunnel large enough to walk through, near Tsusiat Point. After another detour over the point you can walk the remaining 1.5 kilometres on the beach to Tsusiat Falls.

These falls, fed by Tsusiat Lake, are the highlight of the West Coast Trail. They're wider than they are high and they cascade down an 18-metre drop to the sandy shore. It's a popular spot, a destination for many hikers who want to walk only part of the trail. It can become crowded in summer.

Steep ladders climb from the beach to the trail and a bridge crosses the river above Tsusiat Falls. The trail continues through the forest to the Klanawa River, a wide stream with a cable car crossing high above the water. There's a nice campsite near the mouth of the river but beware of incoming tides.

Tsusiat Falls

165

Darling River waterfall

Klanawa River to Michigan Creek

Distance: 9.8 kilometres

The West Coast Trail from the Klanawa River runs mainly through the forest to Michigan Creek but you can walk almost all the way along the beach as long as tides are below 3.6 metres. About 2.5 kilometres from the Klanawa River an old anchor marks a path up to the main trail. As you head toward Michigan Creek you'll pass a derelict donkey engine and grader. A viewpoint overlooks the site where the iron steamship *Valencia* ran aground in January, 1906.

Just under a kilometre past the viewpoint, near the mouth of Trestle Creek, you may see an anchor, parts of the hull and fittings from the four-masted steel barque *Janet Cowan*. She ran aground in December, 1895 in wind and driving snow. Three of her 29-man crew drowned while getting ashore and the captain, cook and two others died of hypothermia within a week. Thirteen survivors were picked up on the 10th day ashore and nine others were picked up later at Carmanah Point Lighthouse.

There's a bridge across Trestle Creek and after about 750 metres another bridge crosses Tsocowis Creek. Just beyond the second bridge a path leads to the beach where there's a nice campsite. You can continue along the shore to the mouth of the Darling River and camp on the beach, downstream from a pretty waterfall. A cable car crosses the river.

A boiler and machinery from the steel steamship *Uzbekistan* lie near the mouth of the river and can be seen at low tides. The Russian ship was carrying war materials from the west coast when she ran aground in April, 1943. Her crew of 50 made it safely to shore.

Michigan Creek, nearly 1.5 kilometres beyond the Darling River, is named after one of the first wooden steam schooners to ply northwest waters. She struck a reef in January, 1893 and the 25 people aboard got to shore, although one died of hypothermia. A boiler and part of the *Michigan's* shaft and propeller remain on a reef opposite the mouth of the creek. There's a popular campsite here and a bridge across the stream.

Michigan Creek to Pachena Bay

Distance: 11 kilometres

This final stretch of the West Coast Trail is also the easiest stretch. The trail, once a supply road for Pachena Point Lighthouse, is wide and smooth compared to the rest of the trail. Headlands between Michigan Creek and Pachena Bay are impassable so you have to stick to the trail. There are, however, several accesses to nice beaches.

Pachena Point Lighthouse was established in 1907, the same year construction of the lifesaving trail began. You'll pass its tidy grounds and white-sided, red-roofed buildings with their commanding views over the surrounding seas. About 700 metres beyond the lighthouse is the Flat Rocks viewpoint where about 100 or 150 Steller's sea lions haul out for winter and early spring. Occasionally 400 or 500 sea lions arrive at the rocks, stay a few days or weeks and move on.

About halfway between Pachena Point and the head of the trail, Seabird Rocks sit 2 kilometres offshore. These isolated islets are a nesting colony for about 2,000 seabirds. As you approach the end of the trail you'll likely encounter day hikers. The first 9 kilometres of the West Coast Trail to Pachena Point are popular among people who want a taste of what the trail has to offer without having to endure the entire 72 kilometres.

Trail viewpoint

CANOEING THE NITINAT LAKES

The Hobiton-Tsusiat watershed, on the western side of Nitinat Lake, has become one of southern Vancouver Island's most popular canoe routes. Although there's less than 17 kilometres of paddling water from the start of the journey in Nitinat Lake to the south end of Tsusiat Lake, the trip, with one or two back-bending portages, takes three to five days.

Like the West Coast Trail, the Nitinat Lakes expedition is a wilderness trip. Proper preparation is required to deal with the possibility of mishaps far from civilization. There are hazards here: it's not a place for little kids or neophyte backpackers in poor physical condition. It's a test of tolerance and strength and canoeists may be forced to paddle against strong winds in Nitinat Lake and carry heavy boats and packs over slippery, muddy trails between lakes. But also like the West Coast Trail, those who come prepared reap the rewards of their efforts.

Getting There — Logging Roads to Nitinat

A gravel logging road to Nitinat Lake begins at Youbou, a village on the north side of Cowichan Lake. Youbou can be reached by taking the Lake Cowichan turnoff from Vancouver Island's Highway 1, about three kilometres north of the city of Duncan.

Nearly 25 kilometres from the start of the gravel road is an intersection. A campground to the left can be used if you arrive too late to begin paddling. The best launching point, at Knob Point on the northwest end of the lake, is reached by turning right at the intersection and crossing a bridge over the Nitinat River. About 2 kilometres from the bridge, turn left at a junction, and a short way down the road, cross another bridge over the Little Nitinat River. It's about 8 kilometres to Knob Point picnic site where there's ample parking.

Packing to Portage

Because of the portages in the Nitinat Lakes, canoeists should pack as they would if hiking the West Coast Trail, carrying the same materials. A small stove is particularly important as driftwood in the Nitinat Lakes is not as plentiful as along the West Coast Trail. A sponge is useful to mop up water in the stern of the canoe. The portages are short, but rough, and everything should be stashed in backpacks. You could tie a fishing rod to the thwarts but all gear should be organized for easy packing between lakes — once with packs, again with canoes.

One provincial topographic map, number 92C/NE entitled *Nitinat Lake* at a scale of 1:125,000, shows Nitinat, Tsusiat,

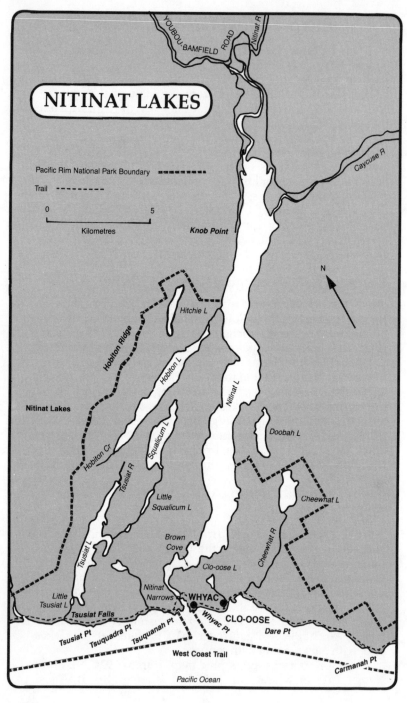

NITINAT LAKES

Pacific Rim National Park Boundary ■ ■ ■ ■ ■

Trail - - - - - - - -

0   5

Kilometres

YOUBOU-BAMFIELD ROAD

Nitinat R

Caycuse R

Knob Point

Hitchie L

Hobiton Ridge

Hobiton L

Nitinat L

Hobiton Cr

Doobah L

Nitinat Lakes

Squalicum L

Tsusiat R

Little
Squalicum L

Cheewhat L

Cheewhat R

Brown
Cove

Tsusiat L

Clo-oose L

Little
Tsusiat L

Nitinat
Narrows

●**WHYAC**●

Tsusiat Falls

CLO-OOSE

Whyac Pt

Dare Pt

Tsusiat Pt

Tsuquadra Pt

Tsuquanah Pt

West Coast Trail

Carmanah Pt

Pacific Ocean

N

170

Squalicum, Hobiton and smaller lakes in the area as well as the main road access into Nitinat Lake. It also shows all of the West Coast Trail. Another provincial topographic map at the same scale shows the same features as well as the rest of Pacific Rim National Park. It's Regional Map 2, entitled *Parksville-Tofino*. The back of the map shows detail on nearby campgrounds and services. Both maps can be purchased from government agents throughout B.C. or by mail. Write to the address on p.177. The maps can be used without a compass but it's wise to carry a compass when venturing into the wilderness.

Nitinat Lake is really a tidal inlet with its outlet about halfway along the West Coast Trail at Nitinat Narrows. Tide tables for Tofino are needed for the courageous few who decide to paddle through Nitinat Narrows, but if you're planning only to canoe on Nitinat Lake as far as the mouth of Hobiton Creek you can get away without them.

The difficulty of the portages in the Nitinat Lakes can't be overemphasized and some canoeists are discouraged from taking the trip because of them. If the water is high enough you can line your boat a kilometre up Hobiton Creek from Nitinat Lake as long as no fisheries closure is in effect. If you must portage, it's nearly two kilometres on a narrow, winding path with numerous hills. Because of the bends in the trail it is usually easiest for one person to pack the boat. Wearing a life jacket helps pad the shoulders. The trail between Hobiton and Tsusiat lakes, about three kilometres, is worse, with generous helpings of mud, exposed tree roots and up-and-down terrain. Canoeists who want to launch their boats on the beach near Tsusiat Falls and paddle back up through Nitinat Narrows will need to portage another kilometre to the West Coast Trail then along the trail to a set of steep ladders down to the beach.

Knob Point to Hobiton Lake

Westerly winds come up on Nitinat Lake around 10 o'clock on summer mornings. You can almost set your watch by the winds and they usually become bothersome, with a heavy chop and whitecaps, shortly after they begin. Although it's less than four kilometres from Knob Point to the mouth of Hobiton Creek, it can be a harrying voyage in the wind. There are few places to pull out before Hobiton Creek so get an early start. The beach at the mouth of the creek is Indian land and permission from local natives is needed to camp on it.

Hobiton Creek, a pretty, winding, one-kilometre stream with deep pools in the upper reaches, usually has a high enough flow to line a loaded canoe up to the lake. There may be a few shallow or swiftly flowing spots, particularly on the lower end. From the mouth of the creek it may appear as if the stream is not suitable for lining a boat, but a short distance upstream conditions improve. Near the top of the creek you'll likely have to paddle across some of the pools.

The portage trail begins about 300 metres past the mouth of the creek on the south side. Look for markers. Distance is slightly less than two kilometres but may take considerable time, depending on the condition of the trail, and the condition of the portager.

Hobiton Lake, seven kilometres long and 800 metres wide at its widest point, lies comfortably in the shadow of Hobiton Ridge, its 750-metre peaks towering over the western side of the lake. Warm summer breezes funnel down the lake: it's a great spot to hoist up a tarp and sail downwind. Hobiton is also a good lake for steelhead and cutthroat trout fishing. Cutthroat, some up to 60 centimetres long, are the best bet. There are also sockeye salmon in the lake. Provincial fishing licences are needed and regulations should be consulted.

There are some nice campsites just beyond the source of Hobiton Creek, along the north side of the lake. Most of the campsites at Hobiton Lake are on the north side, although there is a good one on the south shore at the mouth of a creek near the trail up to Squalicum Lake.

The steep and rugged trail to Squalicum Lake begins about halfway along Hobiton Lake. It's a climb of more than 150 metres over a distance of about 2.4 kilometres. Diehard canoeists could pack a canoe up. Without a boat it's difficult to get a good look at Squalicum Lake but it makes an interesting half-hour hike.

Hobiton mergansers

Hobiton Lake to Tsusiat

The three-kilometre portage trail to Tsusiat Lake begins at the south end of Hobiton Lake where Hobiton Creek flows into the lake. There is no stream between Hobiton and Tsusiat lakes and the only route to Tsusiat is the trail. It's rough and slippery with fallen logs making up parts of the path. There's a pretty swamp along the way and optimistic portagers begin looking for Tsusiat Lake soon after the swamp: unfortunately it's not quite halfway between the two lakes.

Campsites on Tsusiat Lake are not as plentiful as on Hobiton. The best ones are on the western side and there's a nice camping spot near the outlet to the lake. About halfway along the eastern side of the lake a couple of small islands lie in the entrance to a large backwater, an interesting area to explore.

A trail from the outlet at the south end of Tsusiat Lake leads to the West Coast Trail and Tsusiat Falls. Many canoeists meet friends on the trail and spend an evening together on the beach at Tsusiat. Some swap car keys and the canoeists hike home on the West Coast Trail while the hikers return by canoe.

Canoes can be paddled down Little Tsusiat Lake and River toward Tsusiat Falls. How far you get depends on water levels. Those who want to return through Nitinat Narrows can portage down the trail to the falls and along the West Coast Trail to steep ladders leading to the beach.

Tsusiat to Knob Point via Nitinat Narrows

Only the courageous and the crazy paddle through Nitinat Narrows. With tides ripping through at up to eight knots, they are among the most treacherous waters on the coast. Nitinat Bar, with depths of 1.5 metres to 2.1 metres, extends across the entrance to the narrows, creating confused seas and standing waves in adverse weather. Canoeists have drowned here in the whirlpools inside the narrows. The narrows can only be negotiated at slack tides, which last about 15 minutes.

Launching from the beach at Tsusiat may also be a formidable task if the surf is high. If you don't get dumped you're sure to get your feet wet. It's six kilometres from the falls to the mouth of the narrows and paddlers should stay well offshore, particularly around Tsusiat and Tsuquadra Points, to avoid getting chucked against the shore by the surf.

A canoe could be portaged into Nitinat Lake by paddling nearly 3 kilometres beyond the narrows to Clo-oose. You can portage to Brown Cove, in Nitinat Lake on a rough 2.4-kilometre trail from Clo-oose. The trail passes Clo-oose Lake, a good spot to try catching some cutthroat trout. From Brown Cove it's a 17.5-

Seagulls numerous on Tsusiat Lake

kilometre paddle up the eastern shore of Nitinat Lake to the mouth of the Caycuse River and slightly over a kilometre across the lake to Knob Point. Nitinat Narrows is another point on the West Coast Trail where hikers can arrange to meet canoeists.

Canoeists paddling up Nitinat Lake should be mindful of the hazardous winds and plan most of the journey for early morning or evening. There are nice places to camp along the shores of Nitinat Lake near the mouths of streams.

AFTER THE WEST COAST TRAIL, WHAT NEXT?

The West Coast Trail and Nitinat Lakes are the most challenging of Pacific Rim National Park's areas to explore. They require strength and stamina and an ability to take adverse conditions in stride. They are arduous journeys that return as much as they demand.

The other parts of Pacific Rim, however, are no less alluring. They too are places of the sea, and though each possesses unique characteristics, they are bonded by the same ocean.

OTHER BOOKS OF INTEREST

There are a few interesting books about the shipwrecks, history and other features of the Pacific Rim area. Books about seashore life, birds and other wildlife may also be available in local book stores and libraries.

Breakers Ahead, by R. Bruce Scott, Review Publishing House, Sidney, B.C., 1970

Barkley Sound, by R. Bruce Scott, Victoria, B.C., 1972

The Outdoor Idea Book, edited by June Fleming, Victoria House, Publishers, Portland, Oregon., 1978

Drift Fishing, by Jim Gilbert et al, Special Interest Publications, a division of Maclean Hunter, Vancouver, B.C., revised edition, 1985

A Guide to Shipwrecks Along the West Coast Trail, by R.E. Wells, Sooke, B.C., 1981

A Guide to Shipwrecks — Cape Beale to Cox Point, by R.E. Wells, Sooke, B.C., 1984

Shipwrecks of British Columbia, by Fred Rogers, Douglas & McIntyre Ltd., 1973

HANDY ADDRESSES

These addresses may be helpful for people requiring information on tourist facilities, Pacific Rim National Park, the *Lady Rose*, air transportation, fishing licences and regulations, topographic maps, hydrographic charts and tide tables.

Tourism British Columbia,
1117 Wharf St.,
Victoria, B.C.,
V8W 2Z2

Pacific Rim Tourist
   Association,
4586 Victoria Quay,
Port Alberni, B.C.,
V9Y 6G3

Tofino Information Centre,
P.O. Box 476,
Tofino, B.C.,
V0R 2Z0

Ucluelet Chamber
   of Commerce,
P.O. Box 428,
Ucluelet, B.C.,
V0R 3A0

Bamfield Chamber
   of Commerce,
P.O. Box 5,
Bamfield, B.C.,
V0R 1B0

Pacific Rim National Park,
P.O. Box 280,
Ucluelet, B.C.,
V0R 3A0

The *Lady Rose*,
Alberni Marine
   Transportation Inc.,
P.O. Box 188,
Port Alberni, B.C.,
V9Y 7M7

Pacific Rim Airlines Ltd.,
P.O. Box 1196,
Port Alberni, B.C.,
V9Y 7M1

Department of Fisheries
   and Oceans,
3019 4th Ave.,
Port Alberni, B.C.,
V9Y 2B8

MAPS B.C.,
Ministry of Environment,
Parliament Buildings,
Victoria, B.C.,
V8V 1X5

Canadian Hydrographic
   Service,
Chart Distribution Office,
P.O. Box 6000,
Sidney, B.C.,
V8L 4B2

INDEX

ABOUT THE AUTHOR

Bruce Obee is a Vancouver Island writer who specializes in outdoors, travel and environmental topics. He began a freelance career in 1977 after five years in the news business as a reporter for *Victoria Times*, editor of the *Sidney Review* and staff correspondent for the Canadian Press in Victoria. His articles are published by *Beautiful British Columbia* magazine, *Nature Canada, Canadian Geographic, Alfred Hitchcock's Mystery Magazine, The New York Times, Toronto Star, Vancouver Sun* and numerous other North American publications. Some of his writing is published in high-school and university textbooks.

He is winner of the Tourism British Columbia Travel Writers Award and the Western Magazine Award for writing in the out-doors/recreation field.

An avid canoeist, hiker, bicyclist, boater and angler, he lives in Brentwood Bay with his wife, Janet Barwell-Clarke, a marine biologist, and his daughters, Nicole and Lauren.